The Miseducation of Black Children

by Kmt G. Shockley, Ph.D.

Foreword by (Egun) Asa G. Hilliard III, Ed.D.
and Dr. Na'im Akbar

First Edition, First Printing

Front cover illustration by Harold Carr, Jr.

Printed in the United States of America

10-Digit ISBN #: 0-913543-14-4
13-Digit ISBN #: 978-0-913543-14-6

Dedication

To those who work with Black children, especially teachers.

Acknowledgments

No project can be successfully completed without the help of countless people in the community. This work would not be possible were it not for the help of God, the ancestors, my family, my wife Michelle, my friends including Doug, Terence, Tshango and the Boston crew, Rona, Joy, Kamau, Brandon, Osofo, Hope, the Jacksonville crew including Dr. Gray, Bro. Katembo and the 11:00 crew, Nokee, Bryan, Kobie, Leslie, and countless others. Thank God for the guidance of mentors such as the late Nana Baffour (who was around during the entire writing project, at times physically, and at times not physically); Baba Agyei, Mama Akua, Baba Sanyika, Mzee Hannibal Afrik, and the entire Ankobea family including the ALTR family; Dr. Teresa Pope and the South Carolina family, including Aunt Bev and Papa Pope. Drs. Rona Frederick and Joy Banks always offer insights and perspectives that move good works to greatness. Thanks to my faculty friends at George Mason University for all of your critiques as well as your compliments! Thanks to all those who understand and support the works of those of us who are up-and-coming scholars and who promise to continue the legacy that was initiated by our ancestors.

Contents

Foreword by Asa G. Hilliard III   v i i
Foreword by Na'im Akbar   x

Chapter 1   **The Grounding**   1
*Background: Why African-Centered
Education?
The Critical Need for Afrocentric
Education
Concretized and Institutionalized
Miseducation
How Miseducation Happens
Purpose*

Chapter 2   **The Afrocentric Framework**   25
*Theory & Practice
The Miseducation of White People
The Miseducation of Teachers
The Miseducation of Black People
The Need for Re-Africanization
The "American" Concept*

Chapter 3   **Literature**   39
IDENTITY
PAN AFRICANISM
AFRICAN AMERICAN CULTURE
BLACK NATIONALISM
COMMUNITY CONTROL
THE CALL FOR EDUCATION
AFROCENTRIC EDUCATION
THE AKAN EXAMPLE
AFRICAN HUMANISM

Chapter 4   **An Important African Story**   75
Getting to Know Darnell Culturally
Darnell Meets Mama LuLu
The African Story Continues
A Second Great Migration
Africans vs. Niggers
Transformations
Implications

Chapter 5   **Where Do We Go from Here?**   1 21
African Teacher Shortage
Parents Are Miseducated
Establishing Schools
Solutions

Bibliography   1 30

Foreword

Great Africans like Martin Delaney, Yaa Asantewaa, John Henrik Clarke, Stephen Bantu Biko, W.E.B. DuBois, Ayi Kwei Armah, Marimba Ani, Chinweizu, Amilcar Cabral, Yosef Ben Jochannan, Jacob Carruthers, and many others have looked into the deep well of African cultural traditions and have understood the prime foundation of it. Although they expressed it in various ways, it, these great, conscious Africans understood that our culture is the source of our bonds as Africans, our connection to each other, and even to the whole cosmos from that central reality. Our greatest elders mastered the ways of creating nurturing environments for the preservation, growth, development, and intergenerational transmission of that culture as food for our essence as a people.

Our culture encompasses the whole complex of creative experiences that are the product of our study of and response to our divine essence and environmental challenges. Carefully considered, it is a thing of enormous beauty, a thing that makes us whole. Without it, we die. We disappear as a people.

In the words of Ayi Kwei Armah, our "two thousand seasons" of challenge range from our various exploiters from Asia and Europe and include expeditions into Africa and its diaspora, where both physical and cultural genocide were committed, including assaults on our ability to transmit our culture intergenerationally.

Our greatest challenges in response to these assaults are those concerning recapturing control of our structures for intergenerational cultural transmission, restoring our sense of self, and regaining our experience of wholeness. The honorable tradition of the Jele/Jelimuso ("griots") gives us models for performing the essential functions of keeping memories, transmitting values, and providing the basis for evaluation of our current condition. These things do not happen by accident.

One of my greatest joys has been to come to know many among the waves of young Africans who are worthy replacements for our venerable elders and ancestors. Moments of extreme challenge to our survival are marked by betrayal, forgetfulness, family disintegration, and confusion. Pessimists have appeared among us to declare that our young people are a "lost generation" and that our community no longer is capable of giving birth to warriors who hear the high calling of our ancestors and the spirit of our people, who show courage, genius, a sense of mission and purpose, with an uncompromising commitment to continue the struggle. That declaration is far from the truth. On the contrary, we see the continuation of the excellence of our mastery tradition among some of our younger scholars.

This book is evidence that in two critical areas a young scholar has taken up the challenges and is breaking new ground. The first of those challenges is to grasp the African story that is now found in a vast body of scholarship on African history and culture, including especially the seminal works produced during the last few decades on Africa and its diaspora. The second challenge is to follow African traditions of "good speech" by communicating truthfully and clearly these profound ideas and information to the masses of our people, blending the crafts of historian and playwright.

It is not easy for many among us to understand why Africans today should care about ancient Nile Valley civilizations when we have our own pressing survival problems. Many will wonder as well, why we even need ancient history: what possible connection can there be between East Africa and West Africa? And of course, many will wonder what Africa has to do with its descendants in other parts of the world who have been separated from the continent for many centuries. To meet these doubts, the facts of history and culture must be shown to have contemporary global meaning. The global African family must always remain conscious of itself.

Awareness of history and culture and of the global African family alone will not solve all of our problems as a family. However, it is certain that without that awareness, collective action in politics and economics, locally and globally, will fail.

This book is an important contribution to the essential awareness needed by the African family. This book lets us know that our offspring will not let us down. Let Tehuti be satisfied.

(Egun) Baffour Amankwatia II
(The late) Asa G. Hilliard III
May, 2005

With great substance and meaningful applicability, Dr. Kmt Shockley in this document has made a useful corrective contribution to the centuries old problem of improperly educating black children. With his insightful scholarship and thorough research he offers a well-documented and pedagogically correct tool to assist anyone who is committed to following the ancient dictum to help black children to know themselves in order that African people might be restored in their capacity to offer intellectual leadership for all of humanity.

Dr. Na'im Akbar

CHAPTER 1: The Grounding

Background: Why African-Centered Education?

1948 U.S. presidential candidate Strom Thurmond said that there were not enough troops in the U.S. army to integrate Black children into America's public schools. Obviously, Senator Thurmond was not prophetic in his statement; however, he did express the sentiment of a large number of U.S. citizens of that era.

Before 1948, Blacks were not allowed to attend K-12 schools or university institutions that were attended predominantly by European Americans because the nation operated via de jure (by law) and de facto (in reality) racism/white supremacy. De jure racism was established when the U.S. Supreme Court decided in Plessy vs. Ferguson in 1896 that separate but equal institutions and facilities were constitutional. The 1954 Court overturned the 1896 Court's ruling in the Brown vs. Board of Education case, stating that separate educational facilities were inherently unequal.

The 1954 Court's ruling invited desegregation, but desegregation was "used" and interpreted in many different ways. For example, one major "mainstream utilization" of desegregation was to integrate Blacks into American society. To many in the Black community, desegregation was a process of removing racism from social and political processes, such as dismantling "Whites only" and "Coloreds only" educational institutions. That is, Blacks wanted to end the use of mandated separate facilities and institutions.

De jure desegregation has occurred for the most part; however, integration has accompanied it. Integration is viewed by Claude Anderson (2001) as an assimilation process. During the era of segregation, Blacks were forced to build educational institutions in their own communities.

With Blacks being assimilated into the larger European American culture, Black led educational

1

institutions have been diminished. Assimilation, as opposed to desegregation, makes it seemingly unnecessary to have "White only" and "Black only" educational institutions. As a result of the attempts to assimilate Blacks, many of the educational institutions that Blacks established during the period of segregation were lost.

Upon losing the Black founded, administered, and interested organizations, due to assimilation as opposed to desegregation, many in the Black community began to notice some negative effects on the Black children who were being integrated into schools with Whites. They also began to notice Black children suffering from the past negative effects of segregation. For example, Kenneth Clark's (1954) study of the psychological effects of racism on Black children demonstrated that Black children believed themselves to be unattractive.

Gunnar Myrdal (1949) points out the following inequities in American public schools: "Blacks often experience inferior buildings and equipment...Black teachers get lower rates of pay, Blacks have little control over their schools, many common academic subjects are not offered in Black secondary schools" (p. 58).

James Coleman's (1966) *Equality of Educational Opportunity* report found that "...White teachers work in predominantly Black schools, but seldom do Black teachers work in White schools" (p. 1). He also pointed out that "...twelve years after the Supreme Court decision of 1954, America's public schools remain unequal" (p. 1). The aforementioned studies by Clark, Myrdal, and Coleman are examples of some of the issues that many Black and other scholars and activists perceived Black children to be experiencing.

Still another group of scholar-activists held the belief that Black children were experiencing issues that were part of a larger systematic problem being experienced by Black people as a whole. For example, Blacks faced a harrowing range of social ailments that stem from racism: they were harassed by police officers, lynched, castrated, raped, and denied access to adequate health care, housing, economics, justice, labor, law, and politics. The group of scholar-activists with this viewpoint believes that Black children suffer from the same social ailments stemming from racism, and when such ailments manifest themselves in education, Black children suffer educationally. Simply put, when racism and bias manifest in education, Black children suffer.

This group of scholar-activists, those believing that Black children's educational challenges are simply part of a larger group of challenges that Black people face, established educational institutions designed to address the challenges Black children face in education. They wished to develop "Pan Africanist minded" Black children, equipped with the skills to control the psychic and physical spaces that Black people call theirs, and reconnect with (more usable and appropriate) African cultural frameworks as a way to (1) advance the worldwide Black cultural community by advocating the values of African centeredness, and (2) escape from the throes of White supremacy by transmitting a sense of African agency to students.

Early attempts to salvage Black children came in the form of "Freedom Schools," which were established by Blacks who were interested in offering true education to Black students. The Freedom Schools movement was challenged by the fact that schools were largely funded by non-private sources. Schools such as Harlem Prep were able to "demonstrate that the public schools have failed bright Black students," however, "...the failure of these schools was hastened by the loss of corporate money and their remaining peripheral [that is, marginal] to the public school system" (Doughty, 1979, p. 80).

Another attempt to salvage Black children was the community control movement. "The community control movement brought the first introduction of incipient Black

3

Nationalism into the public schools of America" (Afram Associates, 1968, p. 7). The Black Nationalist movement led to the movement for independent Black schools. Doughty points out that four major conferences facilitated the growth and development of independent Black schools: the California Association for Afro-American Education and Nairobi College Workshop (August, 1970); the First Congress of Afrikan Peoples (September, 1970); the First New York City Afrikan-American Teachers Convention (April, 1972); and the Founding Sessions of the Council of Independent Black Institutions (CIBI) (June, 1972). Doughty reveals the historical significance of the CIBI Founding Sessions:

> On June 30, 1972, the Founding Sessions of the Independent Black Institutions was opened in Frogmore, South Carolina. The first CIBI Work Meeting was held at Penn Community Service, Inc., a Black institution in rural South Carolina. The theme of the session was "Making Excellent Education a Reality for Our Youth." Five goals were identified for the new organization: (1) to make CIBI the political vehicle through which a qualitatively different people are produced; (2) to establish a reputation for CIBI as being dedicated to excellence; (3) to charge CIBI with the responsibility of developing the moral character of its students, parents, and staff; (4) to establish CIBI as a source of well-reasoned leadership in the struggle for freedom and internal community development; and (5) to have within CIBI the structural capacity to act upon our continuing responsibility to the majority of our children who are still in the public schools. (p. 87)

The ideological foundations of CIBI are "based on an understanding of and commitment to practice Kawaida, Black Power, Black Nationalism, and Pan Africanism" (Doughty, 1979, p. 97). The African-centered independent Black institution was a vastly different type of institution from an American public school. Some Afrocentric educators held to the belief that the goal of independent Black institutions was not to reform public schools, but to pick up where Africans left off before the European invasions of Africa. That is, Afrocentric educators wished not to develop Black children who, for example, were competitive with White children academically, but to prepare Black children for the tasks they must tackle as members of the larger worldwide African cultural community.

A major goal of the independent Black institution was to transmit African-centered values to children of African descent, and thereby make them "new," qualitatively different people, ready and able to qualitatively change the Black community, That is, they wished to make Black children agents for nation building. CIBI is still attempting to offer Black children an African-centered education.

The CIBI movement began in 1972, and Black children continue to face the problem of cultural mismatch between themselves and the public schools they attend. Further, the Black community continues to struggle in all areas of people activity. Two important question follow: (1) What is African-centered education? (2) How are the values of African-centered education deduced from African culture and transmitted to African children within these schools and to African adults in the communities to achieve the desired end result, which is nation building? Obviously, such understandings may inform us how such educational practice can lead to further the growth and development of Black communities. This book addresses such questions.

The Critical Need for Afrocentric Education

Perhaps the most frightening education problem that Black children and communities face is not the fact that Black children are suffering greatly in U.S. public schools. Perhaps the most frightening problem is not even the glaring gap between Black and white SAT scores (NCES, 2005). Perhaps the greatest problem is not even that Black children in U.S. schools are disproportionately placed into special education classes (Shockley, 2004). Maybe the alarming statistics that Black students only represent 17% of the total U.S. school population yet they are 36% of the students who get suspended from school and represent 32% of the students who are expelled from school (U.S. Department of Education Office of Civil Rights, 2002) aren't even the crux of the problem. Could it be that the aforementioned should be re-conceptualized as hopeful and promising rather than dangerous and perilous?

Will teachers, principals, education researchers, parents, and other stakeholders ever understand that the complex ways in which Black children perform in schools (and in society to some degree) are part and parcel of a necessary defiance against educational content that is woefully inconsiderate of their cultural ontology? Such questions are important for all of us to ponder, especially since many scholars have pointed out that the biggest problem that Black children face is a mismatch between the culture of Eurocentric schools and African (i.e., Black) cultures (Akoto, 1992, 1999; Lomotey, 1992; Shujaa, 1994).

An example of what happens as a result of the cultural mismatch is evidenced in research indicating that Black students continue to linger behind their white counterparts (NCES, 1999). Lomotey (1992) explains that "...the academic achievement of a large number of Black children across the country – as measured by standardized achievement tests, suspension rates, special education placement rates, and dropout rates—has deteriorated considerably over the last twenty years" (p. 455). According to Afrocentric scholars, the problem of the mismatch between Black cultures and the culture "offered" and to be adhered to in schools is cause for complete socio-educational change

6

for Black children and communities. So while Afrocentric educators believe that cultural mismatch is the significant problem for Black students, mainstream education leaders continue to focus on symptoms (such as mainstream notions of academic achievement).

However, academic achievement (as it is usually referred to, e.g., test scores, IQ tests, etc.) is to Afrocentrics what, for example, school violence is to the mainstream education community. That is, the mainstream views school violence as a problem that is birthed from mounting societal problems and issues – such as parenting issues and the ineffectiveness of the criminal justice system—in other words, it is a symptom. Afrocentrics view mainstream notions of academic achievement similarly – as a problem that is rooted in issues of cultural mismatch and racism/white supremacy. Many in the mainstream believe that school violence is best solved by addressing the home/social problems of young people, not by making them prisoners at school. Afrocentrics suggest more holistic approaches, such as understanding academic achievement as an issue that is best addressed by applying a Black (African) culture to Black students, not by attempting to find best teaching practices, but by bringing the academic achievement problems into context, which requires addressing issues of cultural mismatch and racism/white supremacy.

Interestingly enough, however, there is evidence to suggest that Afrocentric schools more effectively reach Black students. For example, the study by Cherry and colleagues (2004) sought to explore the outcomes of Afrocentric education and philosophy on 5th and 6th graders. The results of their research indicate significant positive program effects on the young people who were exposed to Afrocentric education and philosophy. Also, research studies have been conducted—and positive effects found—on the Afrocentric approach to the general mental health of African American adolescent girls (see Constantine, 2006). Additionally, as in the case of Chick Elementary Charter School in Kansas City, Afrocentric education has been used to take students from educational depression to educational excellence, specifically "African American students at Chick see themselves as leaders, and their standardized test scores exceed the average for the state of Missouri" (Christian Science Monitor, 2006).

Considering the above, it is important that African Americans support African centered schools. But the amount of support that African Americans actually demonstrate toward Afrocentric schools has not been measured for some 20 years by researchers. However, an *Ebony Magazine* readers' poll (from 1993) revealed that 93.7% of Blacks support Afrocentric education (in Hotep (2001), p. 18). Even if a scientific poll were conducted today, it would be difficult to ascertain how much actual support there is for Afrocentric education on the part of African Americans because of what Asante (1998) describes as the "mental dislocation" of African people:

> The psychology of the African without Afrocentricity has become a matter of concern. Instead of looking out from one's own center, the non-Afrocentric person operates in a manner that is negatively predictable. The person's images, symbols, lifestyles, and manners are contradictory and thereby destructive to personal and collective growth and development. (Asante, p. 1)

To explain, in discussions and dialogues with African Americans who are concerned about the continuous failure of the American educational system with regard to Black children, they will often state the necessity of Afrocentric education when whites are not present but will hesitate when whites are present. Such behavior creates major problems for proponents of Afrocentric education, especially in terms of the need for support of policies that could help to move toward instituting Afrocentric education and/or some elements of it, which would help Black children. However, African American parents who do have their children enrolled in Afrocentric schools appear pleased with the outcomes, as the majority of parents (over 75%) re-enroll their children in such institutions yearly (Hotep, 2001).

Even though enrollment within private Afrocentric schools has stabilized over the past 10 years, some private Afrocentric schools have lost their independence and become charter institutions. The move from private to "public charter" creates less financial hardship for schools that do so. Examples of such moves from private to public charter are KIMA (aka Kamit Institute) in Washington, DC, and African Centered Education School (formerly Chick Elementary) in Kansas City, MO.

Some Afrocentric schools started as private institutions but now have public charter components added to them, e.g., New Concept Private/Betty Shabazz Charter in Chicago, IL, and Roots Private School, which exists in addition to Roots Public Charter in Washington, DC. However, some Afrocentric schools have maintained their independence for decades, e.g., Nationhouse Watoto and Ujamaa Shule both in Washington, DC, and Hofi ni Kwenu in St. Louis, MO. Discussions and debates continue related to whether or not public and/or charter schools can be truly Afrocentric, considering that they are not independent.

Concretized and Institutionalized Miseducation

Afrocentric education is necessary because much of what parades as education in the West is actually mere political and cultural hegemony, inculcation, and training. Could it be that Blacks who have made it through the levels of academe (from kindergarten "diplomas" to Ph.D.s) feel

9

that since *they* did *it*, *it's* not only possible to do, but *it should* be done? That is, are those of us who finished our diplomas and degrees and should know better, actually harboring feelings of accomplishment? And does that sense of accomplishment disallow us from being able to properly disarm a system of miseducation that has created "comfortable slaves" who would rather advocate for Black children to simply do better in that system rather than to deem it a system of total miseducation and call for replacing it with a system where Black children's education is centered on Black children and their community?

Why do so many people of African descent question African-centered education while doing little to understand it and make sure it is operationalized in Black communities? Are education researchers beholden to a system that they instead should be scrutinizing to make sure it is not harming more Black children? The answers to those questions are difficult ones, but I would like readers to ponder them. But perhaps a starting point for understanding the dilemmas is to shed some light on the history of how the white supremacist creators of the Western academic canons have viewed Black people, and how such views now permeate the K-12 educational system. It is important to note that nothing precludes Blacks from consciously or subconsciously buying into the following notions.

The famous philosopher David Hume writes that Blacks have never had any "ingenious manufacturers amongst them, no arts, [and] no sciences" (1753, footnote). While the historical record proves otherwise, Hume is still considered by some to be one of the greatest minds in history. He is taught to unsuspecting college undergraduates as if his works are unbiased. Most teachers and other college graduates are forced to read Hume while in college; however, in reference to Blacks, Hume believed that they were ignorant and non-contributing. While college professors who teach Hume may never discuss the above quote, the essence of miseducation at the college level comes in the form of not explaining that Hume was obviously ignorant of Black people's immense contributions to the world.

Professors of Western civilization who teach Hume do just as Hume did, and most often leave Black philosophers (who both influenced and participated in the creation of Western civilization) off the syllabus and can find no reason to discuss the Black philosophers who laid the foundation for Western philosophy (such as Amenemhat (1991 B.C.) and Ptah Hotep (2414 B.C.). Also, those Black philosophers who have been some of the most ardent deconstructionists of Eurocentric Western civilization, such as Diop (1981) and Asante (2002), are rarely if ever discussed in the academy, and when they are, their central arguments are dismissed and made into "controversial" euphemisms.

In his *Animal Kingdom* a European writer named Georges Curvier stated that "The African manifestly approaches the monkey tribe. The hordes of which this variety is composed have always remained in a state of complete barbarism" (1935, p. 12). Curvier was by no means an inconsequential figure in history. He is credited as the founder of paleontology, botany, and comparative anatomy. But not only is Curvier's statement about Blacks academically incorrect, it becomes easier to see why, again, Black writers and scholars are left out of syllabi within colleges and universities—because all too many of the founders of contemporary Western education (in the broad sense) and philosophy blocked the knowledge of African contributions by accepting racist dogma.

It is important to note that higher education sets the example for K-12 education. The intellectual venom of Hume, Curvier, and countless others (such as 18th century writers Wilhelm von Humboldt and Alexander von Humboldt who created racial hierarchies) has seeped into the DNA of the academy, and hence, their notions and ideas have impacted what those who work in the K-12 realm are able to do from a "research based" perspective. That is, anti-Black beliefs and sentiments are as much a part of the academy as lectures and exams, and anti-Black beliefs are part and parcel of the miseducation that students receive. When Black college students speak up, they often say that they wonder if their white classmates imagine them to be "monkeys" or other non-intellectual beings. Meanwhile, Black academicians bemoan white and other non-Black students constantly second-guessing their expertise. They also resent their White colleagues constantly raising questions about the necessity of classes and/or research on Black topics. All of this anti-Black fervor started in antiquity when Africans first began to lose wars to Europeans and Asians (see Williams, 1987).

Consider an intellectual contemporary of Hume and Curvier, none other than the famous psychologist Lewis Terman, one of the creators of intelligence tests such as the Stanford-9. Terman continues the debasement by asserting that "The fact that one meets [feebleminded individuals] with such frequency among Indians, Mexicans, and negroes suggests quite forcibly that the whole question of racial differences in mental traits will have to be taken up anew and by experimental methods. Children of this group should be segregated into special classes and be given instruction which is concrete, and practical" (1916, p. 48).

Interestingly enough, professor Terman's wishes have become the command of the current educational establishment. Experimental methods are in place, ranging from myriad "programs" within schools, which are always tried on Black children first, to the disproportionate numbers of Black children in special education classes, evidencing what is often an attempt to further segregate "certain" children based on their "intellectual prowess" and/or ability.

Others (such as Carl Brigham, Edward Thorndike, Robert Yerkes, etc.) also created tests such as the SAT and the IQ, but these men were admitted eugenicists, meaning that they believed in the genetic superiority of people of European descent (Spring, 2005). The legacy of those white supremacists has created the need not just for reformed understanding of race, but for honest dialogue about the nature of the system, which includes the revelation of white supremacy, which undergirds the academic disciplines and must be completely deconstructed in order to understand why Black children are suffering in schools.

Anti-Black sentiment was advanced by scholars, such as the von Humboldts at the University of Gottingen, and was concretized by Princeton University professor Carl Brigham, who in 1925 argued that "immigration should be carefully controlled to safeguard the 'American Intelligence'" (p. 69). However, Brigham did not stop there. The esteemed professor said that he believed "negroes" to be by far the most intellectually inferior race. Later, just before he passed away, he admitted that his "studies" were fallacious. But it was too late. He and the legacy of his intellectual ancestors, such as Hume and Curvier, and his contemporaries, such as Terman, had already done the damage. To date, Brigham's SAT has only changed in form. It has not changed in essence.

Herein are not *excuses* for the trouble that Black children and communities continue to face at the hands of a so-called education system, but are instead the *reasons* why children of African descent must have an African-centered education. People of African descent who advocate for reformed education as opposed to African-centered education no longer have an excuse for such a position. It is primarily the responsibility of African (Black) adults to help make African-centered education prevail for children of African descent.

To continue arguing for reform with knowledge of entrenched white supremacy within the educational system is to advocate for a form of mild mental molestation of Black children. That is, reformers do not realize that white supremacy has permeated the educational system in ways that make that system unsalvageable. African-centered education must immediately be enhanced, supported, and endorsed by the entire community.

How Miseducation Happens

Perhaps the most frightening problem is not trying to figure out what to do about Black children who do poorly in schools and on tests. Perhaps the most frightening problem is demonstrated in the form of a question: *What does it mean for a Black child to perform well within a school system and on standardized tests that are historically and inherently designed to prove and maintain white supremacy?*

Much evidence exists to support the fact that many school systems are culturally biased toward whites and away from Blacks and other groups of children (Sleeter, 1996; Watkins, 2001). There is also evidence that suggests that schools are white supremacist in their cultural orientation (Asante, 1991; Cress-Welsing, 1991; Sleeter, 1994). For Black children, this means that schooling is a process of becoming inculcated with ideas, content, and perspectives that relate to people of European descent, while few to no ideas, content, or perspectives relate to the experiences of people of African descent.

For example, I reviewed a typical 5th grade social studies textbook used in the Washington, DC, public schools in 2008. That book is called *Social Studies. The United States: Civil War to Present.* I reviewed the book to see if any present-day issues related to Blacks were discussed. First of all, few were included. I found a reference to Hurricane Katrina, which is briefly mentioned three times in the book. The 5th grade book states the following after describing when and where Hurricane Katrina occurred:

The Grounding

"People around the country and around the world offered to help [victims of Hurricane Katrina]. The federal government launched a major rebuilding program in the areas damaged by Hurricane Katrina" (Harcourt, 2008, p. 489). No other information about the hurricane is provided to readers. None! In that same vain, the high school geometry book used within the District mentions the importance of students knowing the Pythagorean Theorem. The book makes no reference to theorems that pre-date that of Pythagoras.

The above examples represent blatant miseducation. In the first example, Black children who use the Harcourt textbook are being taught a *perspective* on historical happenings (and Hurricane Katrina is just *one* example; there are many in that book). The viewpoint that is presented goes directly against any perspective held by self-respecting and/or even "politically conservative" Blacks. Most Blacks watched victims of the government's neglect in New Orleans walking in waist-high water, being passed over by CNN and FOX helicopters, and being intentionally shown before the entire world in the most homely ways possibly. Many Blacks believe that the Red Cross failed miserably. While the Red Cross is able to get food and supplies into the most obscure places and under the most horrific circumstances imaginable (such as during wars and conflicts), "somehow" food and supplies were severely delayed to New Orleans. However, the textbook states the following about the Red Cross: "Red Cross workers handed out food and water to victims of Hurricane Katrina" (p. 177). And that is *all* it says about the Red Cross in relation to Katrina. African American children are being trained/taught *away* from the notions, ideas, and opinions of African American adults.

The majority of Blacks believed that much more could have been done to help Katrina victims. Yet, the social studies textbook evades anything close to a Black perspective and instead seems to include a milquetoast, false, and misleading statement about an extraordinarily important historical occurrence. Slyly, and without Black parents and community members knowing it, Black children who read this are being instilled with a perspective that completely disrespects Black people by not including their perspective on Katrina. To inculcate Black children with a *perspective* (not an education) that does not represent the interest of the Black community is the true essence of miseducation.

Furthermore, such action serves to pit Blacks against one another by planting an unseen "seed" in the minds of Black youth. That seed germinates and portends to create a "generation gap" that will have Blacks wondering in the future why such a gap exists where it came from. These awkward, and yet unnecessary, generation gaps in the Black community are the result of the Black community losing its ability to educate its own children.

Interestingly enough, in the case of the social studies text, miseducation begins at the intersection of job discrimination and academic chauvinism – once again at the academy level. To explain, almost all of the authors, contributors, and consultants of the social studies textbook are European American scholars and/or professors, which again is odd since there are scores of scholars and professors who are not European American yet are equally qualified to assist in the writing of such texts. This appears to be academic chauvinism, which presumes that having a diverse body of writers is either unimportant or must be intentionally avoided for some reason. As a result, the group that has historically determined what children are going to learn is still often the only decision-making group.

It may as well be known that Black scholars often feel that if they *were* invited into the process (and there were a few African American contributors to the 5th grade book), they would only be invited *back* if they did not say (or especially *do*) anything that went against the Eurocentric canon that is always being advanced by official boards and commissions.

16

The Grounding

The aforementioned exemplifies the unspoken policy of "being a good little boy or girl" and represents a very serious reason why racial diversity in employment only works when people know "who they are" and are willing to stand up for the children within their own communities. But the real disaster caused by such activity is that it serves to maintain a system of miseducation that should be hurriedly dismantled, especially for Black children.

In the second example, the mathematics textbook asks students to become familiar with the Pythagorean Theorem. While there is nothing wrong with students learning the "theory of the squared hypotenuse," no Black/African names are ever used to describe anything in mathematics, which is odd since the first mathematical genius was an African. "Pythagorean" derives from the Greek philosopher Pythagoras, who could not have "invented" or come up with that theorem since it was required math for constructing the pyramids, built some 2,000 years before he was even born. Could a people build the massive pyramids of Egypt without knowing that the square on the hypotenuse is equal to the sum of the squares of the other two sides?

Why are the theorems and multi-genius knowledge pools of the famous African philosopher and mathematician Imhotep not studied or known about? Worse than a misnamed theorem is the fact that Africans pre-date European mathematics/science philosophers, and no processes or functions are named after them. This is a blatant example of miseducation by way of omission—Blacks are simply left out. When Blacks are included, it is usually miseducation by way of commission—texts will "start discussing slavery, and leave out any information that can help Black children gain a sense of responsibility and respect for self..." (Lomotey, 1978, p. 25).

After establishing a lopsided system where one group is glorified for having accomplished everything and other groups are mere co-stars, when such imbalances are pointed out by the victims of white supremacy, they are often met with responses such as "what difference does it make what someone's color happens to be?" That question is an intellectual sleight-of-hand because if color does not matter, why is there always one color that is highlighted and glorified? When questions are raised about the cultural hegemony within education, there are affirmative looks and head-nodding. But when papers and perspectives are presented that stand to correct the essence of miseducation, they are ignored by scholars of all colors and creeds and awkward (but sometimes necessary) questions and "concerns" abound.

For example, in relation to African-centered education, many say that they are concerned about "separating the races." But the races are already separated according to the U.S. Census (2000). According to the U.S. Census Bureau, U.S. citizens tend to live in homogenous racial/cultural communities. Another stated concern is about the fact that "the world is not Black, so why would we want to advocate for an African-centered education?" That question presupposes that an African-centered education would simply be a Black version of Eurocentric education. Why would someone think that? Could it be that people are not studying to understand the cultural folkways, mores, and ethos of specific cultural groups but are instead applying the ethos of the dominant group to *all* groups? If so, that is inappropriate behavior, for we must advance cultural knowledge about *all* groups, not just one group. Afrocentrism is not simply the reverse of Eurocentrism.

Eurocentrism omits the perspectives and ethics of other groups from academia while raising the European-descended group above its true pay grade. African-centered education is (by defining who people of African descent are culturally) concerned about the African primarily (which is necessary) but is global in perspective and outreach. It is known that many non-Afrocentric thinkers are skeptical about "blaming white people for everything." But the central person to blame from an African-centered standpoint falls upon the African him/herself. It does not take much reading of African-centered literature to come to understand that Afrocentric writers believe that Blacks should have done a better job protecting their people and their indigenous cultures. Furthermore, they believe that Blacks are responsible for correcting the problems that exist within African (Black) communities. However, African-centered thinkers do understand that European global hegemony took advantage of all of the loopholes Africans left open and exploited Africans for their own advancement.

What is necessary at this moment in the history of African people is for them to find a way to reconnect with who they are as Africans and stop being overly concerned with how others may feel about them becoming reconnected with their indigenous cultural selves. The concern over how other groups of people may feel when a Black person becomes African centered is important to discuss. Often Black people do not want to act in a way that might offend other people from a "racial" perspective (especially white people). However, there is a price for finding within your personality a "*less* African way of being," and that price is paid by the Black community, which cannot advance properly when you do so.

Additionally, for some people of African descent, somehow being intentionally less African in behavior, dress, style, and preference ends up making them behave in a more "PRO everyone else" manner (and especially PRO white), and they may accidentally behave in a more ANTI African way —just to prove cross-racial loyalty. That is, Blacks may become hostile toward one another in an effort to "prove" they are "equal opportunity" people. By equal opportunity, I mean that Black people will often attempt to demonstrate that they feel the same way about all people, "regardless of color." While that seems like a positive attitude, no other groups behave that way (Anderson, 2001). Instead, other groups don't hesitate to compete with Blacks in order to secure a future and a good life for their own children and communities.

African-centered efforts represent the only attempts being made in the Black community to truly secure the future of Black children by mandating that Blacks return to the source of the cultural foundation from which they came, which is indigenous African culture. Besides Blacks, no other group of people sacrifice themselves so that they can be seen as "fair." African-centered education is a critical imperative at this moment in the history of African people. But African-centered people cannot become so "advanced in their thinking" that they "transcend" an ability to stay connected with the struggle to fight for Afrocentric education.

Purpose

The purpose of this book is to provide educators and those who are seriously concerned about the crisis that Black children are facing with some significant histories, stories, and important perspectives that will help to inform them of crucial matters related to the education of Black children. Essentially, education is a process of extracting that which is within children. It is not possible to extract that which is within until there is an understanding of exactly what is within children. This work attempts to provide insight as to what is within Black children.

The Grounding

In attempting to extract what Wilson (1993) calls the natural genius of Black children, it is important to first know who the Black child is culturally. One of the biggest problems we face today is that the Black community has not made a collective decision that they are, in fact, a cultural group of African people. That indecisiveness has set us up to be the world's "puppets and playthings" (Akoto, 1992, p. 4) because as the African ancestors say, "When you don't know where you are going, any road will get you there!" If you do not claim your African self, anyone can come along, tell you who you are, and then get you to fulfill *their* agenda.

This work offers an opportunity for those who are concerned about Black children to gain a reference for understanding the power of being grounded in African culture as well as continental and non-continental African history. Such grounding is a necessary initial step for becoming African centered. This book is especially designed for those who teach and/or are raising or working with Black youth.

Becoming a puppet and a plaything of those who are directed and powerful is an inevitable outcome for a people who have so many members who enjoy claiming any and all parts of existing and potential identities, with the exception of the identity that is so evident in them. The following situation illustrates this very sad point. While teaching my students (all of whom are practicing K-12 classroom teachers) one afternoon, I asked them to sit in groups of four or five and discuss things about "their culture" with one another. I left the topic open because I wanted to see where they would go in the small-group discussions. I wandered around the room listening. One of the groups consisted of four White women and one Black woman. One of the white women in the group said, "Why don't we all go around and say what our culture is! I mean, who *are* we anyway?" She kind of chuckled and started off by saying, "Well, I am Italian and Irish."

Another woman said, "I am German. Both my parents' grandparents were from Germany."

Another woman claimed to be English and Scottish.

The Black woman (a very dark-skinned woman who is a teacher at a mostly Black middle school) reported as follows: "I am American and British."

The White women briefly took a kind of pause that seemed to indicate that later they would be discussing the Black woman's answer with one another. It was as though they wanted to discuss it without her there and without me standing by eavesdropping. When I heard the Black teacher's response that she was American and British, I thought about my facial expression. I wanted to keep a "poker face." What both the White women and I knew was that she was in denial of her own African self.

I just kind of half smiled, nodded, and walked away, wondering how I could positively impact that woman. At the end of the day, I asked two of the white students from that group what they thought about the small group and the things that were said. I asked them separately.

One replied, "Well, it was obvious that Jackie [the Black woman] didn't want to say that she was African or African American."

The other white student said, "Well, I guess some people have some discomfort about being from certain cultures."

I said, "Be specific."

She replied, "I mean, well I guess Jackie just didn't want everyone to know that she was Black. But you can tell she's Black." The student then asked me, "Do you think she means she's Black when she says she's American?"

By way of this exercise, I inadvertently learned a telling fact: The only person in the room who does not realize that Jackie is Black (African), is Jackie! During that exercise, I walked around and heard countless other Blacks reporting their Cherokee, Irish, British, and even "Latino" heritage, rejecting their obvious African heritage. Not one of the Black students that I overheard mentioned Africa to their group mates. Now, years later, I have begun to realize that cultural self-denial is a problem not just for Jackie and my students alone but probably for the masses of Black people.

Many in the Black communities of the United States are uncomfortable with the notion that Blacks are a different "culture" from, for example, whites. Hence, Black teachers often align themselves with the theory that we all are "American," and many teach from that standpoint. Unfortunately, the notion that we all are American sounds good, but it is an incomplete analysis that results in the miseducation of all who hear it (Akoto & Akoto, 1999; Asante, 1988; Hilliard, 1997).

Miseducation as explicated by Carter G. Woodson (1933), is a process that includes victims of racism/white supremacy degrading their intellect and existence while upgrading the intellect and existence of their oppressors. Woodson further explains that oppressed people, such as Blacks, even when not assigned to go through a "back door," will either find or create a back door to go through. The notion that "we all are American" is a much more politically debilitating notion for Blacks than it seems to be on its face; it is in fact the epitome of miseducation.

The problem with the political sentiment that "we are all American" is that it culturally neuters people, but at a greater expense to Blacks since they are more culturally vulnerable than any other group because they have been purposely stripped of their specific cultural self-knowledge. That is, are they descended from the Akan? Ewe? Hausa? From what specific group does a person of African descent come?

Calling oneself "American" is culturally neutering to any group, but in the case of whites, they are, in fact, not simply white or American, they are mostly of European descent and from a specific culture or ethnicity. (Of course, anthropologists point out that whites are of African descent, too, if traced back far enough.) To say that people of European descent are "white," as though they are simply "Americans" whose historical journey starts in the United States, is wrong because it erases their European cultural heritage.

CHAPTER 2: The Afrocentric Framework

Theory and Practice

Afrocentric ideas require a reorientation of thinking on issues pertaining to education because when traditional lenses are used, they are often insufficient tools for understanding Black phenomena (Asante, 1990). For example, Afrocentric educators argue that while multicultural education may be useful, in its current form it compromises the Black community's need to regain some very basic elements, such as the formulation of a sense of African identity. Banks (2001) describes multiculturalism as a reform effort involving changes in content integration, knowledge construction, the formulation of an equity pedagogy, prejudice reduction, and implementing an empowering school culture and social structure within schools (p. 5). Nowhere in Banks' typology is there a discussion of identity—the most critical element facing Blacks today (Hilliard, 1997; Akoto, 1992; Shujaa, 1994; Akoto & Akoto, 1999, 2006, 2007). Murrell (2002) illustrates Afrocentric educationist concerns:

> Multicultural education as it is applied to work with African American children [is problematic] namely, the detrimental influence that a pervasive diversity agenda has when it eclipses the critical identity work that under girds powerful literacy learning for African American children. Knowing about diverse people and experiences should not supersede a child's own understanding of self and culture... (p. xxi).

While Afrocentrics decry many conventional methods that are aimed at "students of color," they are most critical of mainstream/Eurocentric education for Black children because the ideas pose as being "universal thinking laws" while Eurocentric ideas are really largely specific to people

25

of European descent (Ridley, 1971; Doughty, 1973; Madhubuti, 1973; Akbar, 1984, 1992; Lomotey, 1978, 1992; Asante, 1980, 1988; Brookins, 1982; Hale-Benson, 1982; Lee, 1992; Hilliard, 1997; Anderson, 2001). Eurocentric education purports the superiority of analytical thinking; meanwhile, African American educational psychologists offer that African Americans are more relational in their thinking (Hale-Benson, 1982; Nobles, 1994; Hilliard, 1997).

The educational system omits the roles of entire groups who created knowledge while ostensibly suggesting that Blacks should reorient their natural thinking processes. Afrocentric educationists critique Eurocentric universalism. Afrocentric writers also attempt to correct the historical record by bringing the cultural accomplishments, folkways, and mores of Africans to the fore so that Blacks (and others) can learn from those histories.

While Afrocentric education is seen as a "politically charged" endeavor, it is actually no different from what most other groups do to educate their children. For example, Catholics engage students in Catholic-centered education by purporting the primacy of Catholicism; Jewish-centered schools teach students that they should participate in the larger society but pledge primary allegiance to Jewish needs and causes. Asa Hilliard (1997) reported similar activity among Asians and Latinos. African-centered education is similar, only instead of imbuing senses of Catholic, Jewish, Asian, or Latino allegiance, it instills a sense of African allegiance.

Afrocentric education leaders believe that all people, including people of European descent, have been miseducated in a way that Africans (Blacks) are positioned to be "public enemy number one." This has been a problem ever since Europeans began to defeat Africans in official as well as unofficial wars (unfortunately, there is currently an unofficial war between Europeans and Africans). Yet, many have been miseducated to believe that what occurred between Europeans and Africans in the past makes no difference today.

The Miseducation of White People

The discounting of so-called American white people's cultural heritage and past deeds is problematic for several reasons. First, it denies white children the power of knowing who they are; and considering that education is defined as a process of self-discovery, white children are miseducated when history is presented to them as though they are not of European descent. In fact, according to Columbus, white people migrated to the Americas sometime around the late 1400s when he was given permission and funds from the Portuguese government to begin sea exploration. Even though Columbus misconstrued his location, he did eventually make his way to the New World. (Evidence has been found that Blacks had already made their way to the North American continent and had been trading back and forth with the natives of what is now the United States for centuries; see Van Sertima, 1976).

When teachers say that Columbus discovered America, they should clarify that such a discovery was not made for all groups of people. In fact, Columbus discovered America only for people of European descent. To continue teaching that he discovered America as a "universal" fact is miseducation. Columbus and Amerigo Vespucci represent the first Europeans to make their way to the Western hemisphere. Later, other Europeans, such as the families of George Washington and Thomas Jefferson, migrated to North America. They are also the ancestors of some of the white people of Europeans descent in the Western hemisphere today. Many point out that via sexual rape, Washington and Jefferson also have Black progeny (Gordon-Reed, 1997).

The second problem is that ignoring white people's European cultural heritage feeds the global fantasies of white supremacy by causing an apparent disconnect between certain aspects of European history and white Americans. This has caused some history writers to create bodacious tales of European greatness while ignoring the tremendous historical challenges that Europeans faced and, more importantly, the challenges they have caused for other groups of people.

To explain, European history is a full and rich (yet in many ways sordid) history. If the truth were told and European history presented properly, children of European descent would see themselves as part of the European cultural/historical story that includes the Greeks, Polish, Romans, and Napoleon. But instead, history in U.S. schools is usually presented as though there is no cultural connection between current day white Americans and the Crusaders, Greeks, Romans, American chattel slaveholders, Alexander (who, by way of racism, is called "Alexander the Great" – he was not great for all groups of people), Martin Luther, Queen Elizabeth, Bach, Brahms, David Hume, Carl Brigham, and Queen Victoria's ancestors. Since these people are white, European American children may form some connection with them, but such connections are likely to be decoupled because white children are not properly taught the direct ancestral and political connection between themselves and those predecessors.

Unfortunately, white supremacist accounts of history ignore the thievery of the Greeks, the inhumanity of the Romans, and the negative culture-affecting deeds of Napoleon and Alexander. Ignoring and falsely representing the negative aspects of European history adds to the problem of racism/white supremacy because it disallows White children from being able to see themselves as wholly as other people see them. Instead, such omissions and commissions

28

falsely bolster white cultural self-esteem, which is the first ingredient for concocting white supremacy.

The third problem caused by ignoring white people's cultural heritage is related to the second problem. On the one hand, negative aspects of European cultural heritage are often omitted from textbooks, and white children are left to formulate decoupled relationships between themselves and their European historical predecessors. Meanwhile, the truth of matters relating to European history seeps into other cultural communities. Consider the following illustration:

The famous philosopher Plato acknowledged that he was educated by African teachers in ancient Ta Meri (Africa) for 11 years (see Asante, 1990). Such information is not discussed in white communities or in public schools. But among some groups, such as Blacks, that information is becoming more widespread and will soon virtually be "common knowledge." When Blacks repeat certain information, such as the fact that Imhotep predates Pythagoras, miseducated chauvinistic whites become offended; yet proof of the information widely exists. So instead of a discussion about the multi-genius ways of Imhotep, it turns into a "race issue" between Blacks and whites—a race issue that is caused solely because of the miseducation of white children and communities. White children need to know that they are of European descent, and they need to know a much fuller European history.

The Miseducation of Teachers

Perhaps one of the topics that European Americans are most miseducated about is African people (including Black people all over the world). Perhaps one of the oddest fairy tales about Black people in the U.S. is that they largely "sold themselves into slavery." Somehow, some teachers of all cultural groups are trained (miseducated) to believe that the "African kings" sold their own people into slavery so that the kings could become rich. While it is true that in some regions African kings and queens were complicit during the enslavement period, the overwhelming majority of Africans were tricked and many were kidnapped and/or threatened into becoming chattel slaves throughout the Americas. What is most important, however, is that even those Africans who were complicit may not have had a way of knowing that their people would be exported and become *chattel* slaves.

No slavery is good slavery, but chattel slavery (such as U.S. slavery), where a person becomes the sole property of another person and has absolutely no rights, no voice, and their very body belongs to the master and his wife, was unheard of in Africa (Clarke, 1991). There is an enormous difference between historical internal servitude and chattel slavery, which completely knocked the Africans off cultural balance. These two forms of slavery should not be discussed as if they were the same or even related.

One way to reeducate oneself about this matter is to use the European Jewish Holocaust as an example. Considering the magnitude of Hitler's killings and his reach, there were certainly Jews who helped Hitler capture and kill other Jews (some authors even controversially point to the possibility of Jewish financing of Hitler's campaign, Allen, 1971). While a few Jewish people may have been complicit in the killing of six million people, no one says or believes that "the Jews" killed themselves; instead we all realize that Hitler was the culprit. In that same way, a few Africans were complicit, but they were neither the culprits nor the beneficiaries of chattel slavery. No longer should anyone who teaches or reaches a Black child believe that s/he is in the U.S. because his/her own people were practicing slavery themselves and/or that Africans "sold themselves" into slavery.

The Afrocentric Framework

It also should not be overlooked that for most of human history Africans have been in grand leadership on the planet. That is, the fact that Africans are "down and out" now, does not represent the fact that they have spent most of human history as the victors of great wars (such as early ones in Ta Meri/Kmt with the Asians and Europeans). Often, the American educational system's treatment of people of African descent includes no recognition of centuries of African greatness and grandeur, such as the development of the world's first university, the creation of the concept of family life, and the earliest conceptions of the Divine.

What is even more insidious is that U.S. media often portray Black people as being the "niggers" the slaveholders always said Blacks were. For centuries, people of African descent in the U.S. fought against the negative notions about them as being the awful and animalistic people that white supremacy said they were. However, recently the U.S. media have been able to accomplish what simply could not be accomplished in earlier times. The white supremacist U.S. media have finally been able to demonstrate the un-demonstrable. That is, unlike earlier times in U.S. history, the media have been able to find Black people who are willing to behave in extraordinarily embarrassing ways that begin to make the point of the white supremacists.

For example, slaveholders historically had to force Black men to disrespect Black women via the creation of "slave markets," where Black men were forced to sell Black women to white men for sex. Now, it is very easy to find Black men disrespecting Black women (note rap artists such as Flavor Flav, Nelly, and 50 Cent). Slaveholders had to force Black people to give up and laugh at their African names, but now it is more common for a Black person to be amused and turned off by hearing an African name. Entrenched White supremacy is even more evidenced by the fact that the only African names that are not "funny" are the

31

ones that the Eurocentric media deems are okay – such as the name "Barack Obama" (and even he has been ridiculed because of his name). Blacks should have enough self agency to decide that African names are okay ... it should not be that a name / article of clothing / hairstyle / accent (etc) is okay when it becomes acceptable to European Americans. Even though some Blacks cringe when they hear that certain names are European-derived and some names are African-derived, it is true. And furthermore it is unfortunate that because of years of indoctrination, many Blacks prefer to hear European names.

People of African descent have become enthralled by things that are not African, and they strive very much for things that are European or of little true value (such as costume jewelry, overly expensive cars, and trendy clothes). Slaveholders tried to convince Africans that they were inherently violent. For centuries people of African descent protested against this, demonstrating that they were a peaceful people. Now, many mostly Black neighborhoods are rife with violence to the point where elders and children are no longer safe.

What is most important for teachers to understand (regardless of the teacher's cultural background) is that the ways Blacks are portrayed, and even the ways Blacks behave nowadays, *does not represent Black culture.* Many people have equated smoking marijuana, homicide, disrespectful lyrics in music, sagging pants with underwear and hind parts showing, constant cursing, using the word "nigger," using the words "nigga," "bitch," and the "F" word, single parent households, the "down low" dressing according to the latest styles and fashion, and "having an a-ti-tude" with being Black and/or Black culture. However, what is important to note is that Black people are, in fact, Africans (as discussed before). Indigenous African culture did not include any of the nasty behaviors and/or pejorative words and behaviors presented above. In fact, the nastiness and foul behavior in Black communities did not become as pervasive as it is now until *after* Blacks got to the U.S. and other parts of the West. Therefore, those behaviors are Black people's *reactions* to capitalism and westernization, not their truest and most meaningful cultural output.

Children and others are miseducated when they are taught that the negative characteristics outlined above are "just how Blacks are." According to scientists such as Louis and Mary Leakey and Donald Johanson (all of whom are white), Blacks are the patriarchs and matriarchs of human history, and for the most part they ruled peacefully and with a sense of harmony throughout most of human history. If that is the case, then the few years of behaving like non-Africans in the Americas cannot erase the thousands of years of behaving with a sense of immense respect and dignity toward one another. In fact, what is necessary at this moment in history is that Blacks re-Africanize.

The Miseducation of Black People: The Need for Re-Africanization

Black sociologists point out that many of the television programs about Africa do not depict Africans positively. Unfortunately, media seem to oftentimes point to the issues of poverty, disease, and hunger in Africa. In the author's trips to Africa, I note that there is much more to see than the negative – in fact, most of what is to be seen is very positive. Many white researchers have claimed that Africans are unable to have a "culture" because they are too primitive. Researchers (such as Toynbee, 1979) claimed that Africans are close to being non-human, have little to no intelligence, and are in constant need of help from Europeans. On August 21, 1858, President Abraham Lincoln stated in a speech that he "... [had] no purpose to introduce political and social equality between the white and the Black races...." He continued, "There is a natural disgust in the minds of nearly all white people to the idea of an indiscriminate amalgamation of the White and Black races." These kinds of negative comments made about Africans have also been made about Blacks in the United States and throughout the globe. As a result of Blacks having lost wars that they did not realize they were engaged in with Europeans and Arabs, a host of degrading things have been perpetrated against Blacks, and many Europeans have historically seen them as inferior and subhuman. Europeans colonized virtually every country in Africa, forcing Africans to practice alien European cultures, speak foreign languages, turn against their own people, and adopt European religions in place of African culturo-spiritual practices. Europeans aided and abetted African cross-group fighting to the point of causing Africans to commit genocide against one another in some African countries such as Rwanda.

In the U.S., Blacks have experienced similar punishments as Africans in Africa. Blacks in the Western Hemisphere have been made into chattel slaves, barbecued, lynched, castrated, cheated out of their property, beaten by police, discriminated against, purposely mistreated and misdiagnosed by physicians, psychometrically abused, psychologically abused, culturally raped, and even accused of being reverse racists. Reverse racism is a particularly foul game that is played on Blacks. For example, recently several conservative radio talk show hosts have claimed that if Barack Obama were to become president of the U.S., Blacks should no longer say that people of European descent are racist and/or that the U.S. is a racist country. However, what is again ironic is that Blacks (such as Reverend Jeremiah Wright) are referred to as reverse racists, and policies such as affirmative action and reparations are seen as reverse racism. Yet white men have served as presidents of the U.S. since the country's inception.

The Afrocentric Framework

There are many results of the attacks on Black people worldwide. One of the most unfortunate is that many Blacks have themselves become ashamed of being Black (see psychologist Na'im Akbar's *Breaking the Chains of Psychological Slavery*, 1996). In the U.S., educators generally do not contextualize Black suffering in such ways that Blacks can learn the information without becoming ashamed. Oddly enough, educators seem to concern themselves more about creating guilt feelings in whites than creating prideful feelings in Blacks. Furthermore, some educators are even concerned about "angering" Black students, so they choose not to teach contextualized Black history (Wilson, 1990). Not teaching contextualized Black history in such ways that Blacks are empowered by their own cultural/historical story is blatant and overt miseducation, yet it occurs every day in U.S. public schools.

Since information pertaining to Black history is not handled properly in educational arenas such as schools, and since Africans are dehumanized and viewed negatively via media and educational outlets, many Blacks in the U.S. have negative beliefs and sentiments about Africa. The negative beliefs and sentiments are often coupled with cultural self-denial, meaning that Blacks will often claim that their cultural heritage is "complex" or "mixed," to the chagrin of acknowledging that they are African. In classes that I have taught I have asked Black students how they classify themselves. I have heard them claim cultural affiliations including Irish, "Indian" (pre-U.S. Native American), English, and Caribbean. Sometimes I ask them, "Well, what about African?" I have heard responses such as, "Yeah, I'm like 2 or 3 percent African." I have heard, "But see, not all Blacks come from Africa," and so forth. When Blacks deny that they are African, they deny their own cultural heritage, which they would not do if they had fuller knowledge about African history and what it means to be African.

The "American" Concept

In the same way that whites are not really white Americans but are Europeans, Blacks are not really Black Americans—they are Africans. In the United States, both groups are citizens, but neither is American. If Blacks and whites are Americans, then the Native Americans (i.e., "Indians") of this country never really existed. It is chauvinistic to postulate that the natives (who were already here) do not represent the original cultural manifestation of this land. Simply put, to say that Blacks and whites are "American," is disrespectful to the natives of this land (the U.S.) because they had a name and cultural affiliations before European arrivals.

Also, for social justice purposes, it is incumbent upon any conscientious and culturally sensitive person to acknowledge that countless treaties were broken between the Native Americans and the law-breaking Europeans. Each and every time we call ourselves "American" we bastardize all natives—whom many still disrespectfully call "Indians." Furthermore, they are not even "Native Americans" because such a name implies that they agree that this land was "America" prior to European arrivals. Either that or it implies that whatever the native people were doing or whatever they may have called this land before European arrivals is unimportant compared to the current notions and ideas as laid out by Europeans.

Simply because you reside in a country or are born in a country does not mean that it is the country of your ancestral origins. Many in the United States continue to confuse nationality with citizenship. One's nationality is related to one's ancestral lineage.

Also consider the concept of "nationalism" and its root word "nation." Nationalists strongly identify with their political group and often believe that their people represent a "nation that is within a nation." To illustrate, many Jewish

36

people travel back and forth between the U.S. and Israel. Seth, a 34-year-old New York-born Jewish friend of mine travels back and forth between the U.S. and Israel and has family in both places. Even though Seth was born in New York, he refers to himself as a "Jew," not an "American." In fact, Jews represent a nation within a nation in the U.S., and Seth is an Ashkenazi Jew. But he holds United States citizenship.

I have observed Seth telling many people that he is Jewish because he notes an Israeli lineage. I have observed my Latina friend Lisa telling people that she is Latina because her roots are Panamanian. I have observed my Asian friend Marie telling people that she is Asian because her roots are Chinese. No one contests Seth, Lisa, or Marie; however when my friend Darnell tells people that he is African because his lineage is from there, they scowl at him, "Well, from what country then? Weren't you born in D.C.?"

No one asks Seth what part of Israel he is claiming; no one asks Lisa which country makes her Latina; and no one asks Marie from which Asian country she derives.

When people of African descent claim their African heritage as their nationality (as they should), for some reason people seem to be put off. Some Black people who were born in the U.S. adopt African names and wear African clothes. Unfortunately, those simple things (names and clothes) annoy some people in the U.S., including Blacks themselves. I have never seen people scowl at Seth, Lisa, or Marie when they claim their nationality and wear their traditional clothes. People seem to accept Seth, Lisa, and Marie and move on.

When I was in college, I consistently heard my Italian-descended roommate Lyle (who was born in Indiana) refer to himself as Italian, not even Italian American. I never heard anyone question Lyle's Italian-ness. Why is there so much irritation toward Darnell, but none toward my non-African friends? There are two potential reasons why there is so much fervor against the notion of people of African descent reclaiming personal agency and African identity.

The first reason is that, generally speaking, people have become accustomed to African descendants accepting notions and definitions about themselves that did not originate with African people. Often such notions and definitions originated with Europeans. Secondly, little is known about Afrocentric constructs (such as what Afrocentric people mean when they claim an African identity, Pan Africanism, African values, etc.) and how those constructs work in schools. The next chapter explicates African-centered constructs through the prism of literature that has been written over the years and that focuses on explicating African-centered education.

CHAPTER 3: Literature

Toward Understanding Afrocentric Ideas and Education

Courtesy: Shockley, Kmt. (2007). "Literatures and Definitions: Toward Understanding Afrocentric Education." *The Journal of Negro Education,* 76 (2).

It is difficult to state exactly what "Afrocentric education literature" is because there are myriad opinions on how to define such literature. This chapter unveils the literature of Afrocentric educationists who are interested in "cultural reattachment," that is, those who believe that Black children will fare better when they are a part of Black communities that understand the dire need for Blacks to attach to African cultures.

Cultural reattachment Afrocentrists literally suggest that Blacks should choose an African culture to become familiar with and practice that culture in whole or in part. They spell the commonly used Afrocentric with an "I" to produce Africentric because they believe that African culture (not merely a sense of one's cultural Blackness) is a solution for the educational malaise being experienced by Black children. Cultural reattachment Afrocentric educationists believe that the socio-cultural issues within the Black community are antecedents to focusing on the educational issues.

I chose to illuminate the literature of this particular group of scholars for a few reasons. Firstly, many of the writers established schools that have lasted for over twenty years (e.g., Kwame Akoto and Haki Madhubuti); others have proven longevity by having established Afrocentric "schools of thought" (e.g., Molefi Asante and Maulana Karenga). Secondly, while Afrocentric ideologists and educationists lack recognition in the mainstream literature, many of them are very popular and highly regarded within the Black community (e.g., Na'im Akbar, Mwalimu Shujaa, Marimba Ani, and Asa Hilliard) and have been prolific writers and world-renowned lecturers.

Afrocentric education scholars advance several big concepts that constitute the "cultural imperatives" of Afrocentric education. The first cultural imperative of African-centered education is identity. Identity is primary because if the Black child does not know who he or she "is," that child cannot know his or her purpose. Learning who you are necessitates understanding the relationship between you and others. Afrocentric educationists stress the importance of this through a concept called Pan Africanism, the second imperative of Afrocentric education. Pan Africanist ideology is the understanding that all people of African descent are African (Cabral, 1970). This principle is important because it molds the African child together with his community, that is, Pan Africanism teaches the African child that he or she has shared interests with the rest of the African world.

Pan Africanist understanding leads to the important act of using "traditions which affirm you" (Madhubuti, 1973. For the African child, these traditions are present in African/African American culture and are the third imperative of Afrocentric education. Knowing your culture teaches you the values that are a part of your tradition. Many Afrocentric educationists refer to an African axiology—"Njia," a Kiswahili word meaning the way through our values—which is the fourth imperative of African-centered education.

Njia is just one example of an African value system and like other adopted African value systems, is a critical element because it engenders a sentiment for Black nationalism, which is the fifth imperative of Afrocentric education. Once the African child is imbued with a sense of African nationalism, he or she will understand the need to take agency for building and controlling the institutions in the community, which is the sixth imperative of Afrocentric education. Finally, in order for the six imperatives to be transmitted, the African child must be educated, not schooled—the final imperative of African-centered education.

Afrocentric educationists seem to combine Afrocentric ideology and cultural relevancy to produce Afrocentric education. I used Asante's (1988, 1990, 1998) general definitions and explanations of Afrocentric ideology and Ladson-Billings' (1994, 2001) descriptions of culturally relevant pedagogy for assistance to explicate this literature. The imperatives of Afrocentric education provide an explanation of how such scholars understand cultural reattachment through education.

Identity

Wolof, Akan, Dogon, Ewe, Zulu, Hutu, Tutsi, Swahili, Fante, Nubian, Bantu, and others: Who are these African people? The 11 named communities represent 8 different nations. Afrocentric education scholars identify Africa as the true source of identity for Black children. The question of who the Black child "is," is understandably complex, especially considering the fact that he or she may have come from one of the communities mentioned or from another African community. The identity crisis began for African (Americans) as soon as the first slave ship left the African shore. That is, the Black identity crisis has its roots in the chattel slavery experience in America (Akoto, November 2001; Fordham & Ogbu, 2005).

The literature on Afrocentric education ranges from explanations of Black children as Africans in America, in other words, Africans who happen to be in the United States, to African Americans—a group of people who have their

41

roots in Africa but have developed a distinct and unique culture of their own called "African American."

Afrocentric educationist and school Principal Kwame Akoto explained that Black children are simply African because their cultural roots are in Africa. He stated,

> Leadership in our school practice the Yoruba [sic] tradition as a way to inform the cultural direction of the school; however, we do not force that tradition on others, we wish not to use foreign and alienating cultures such as the European/American culture, which continue the diatribe against our children (K. A. Akoto, personal communication, March 2002).

Akoto's idea is that if Black people become acquainted with African cultural traditions, they will be more productive because they are practicing something that is "known" to them rather than completely submersing themselves in the foreign and alienating Eurocentric American culture. Others advance a more general Afrocentric approach. Haki Madhubuti (1973) said ". . . we must choose from the best of African culture and refine and adopt those practices which advance our cause. . . " (p.4). Madhubuti's assertion pertains to the fact that African culture is not "static," and certain practices may no longer be usable. Although Akoto and Madhubuti agreed that Africa is the source and origin for Black people, Akoto uses Yoruba [sic] culture to help inform the direction of his school, whereas Madhubuti applies general Afrocentric understandings, such as the need for Black unity, self-determination, and community building, at the Afrocentric school he leads, which is called New Concept Development Center of Chicago, Illinois.

To address the Afrocentric requirement that keeps African people centered on African culture for the purpose of correctly answering the identity question, Madhubuti's statement about choosing from among the "best practices" of Black people globally, refers Africans moving forward as a people who must choose from the best of what African cultures have to offer. Although Akoto differs from Madhubuti in that he would promote using one frame as "cultural informant" (e.g., Yoruba), he also seems to advance the idea that general Afrocentric practice is best within Afrocentric schools. Both Akoto and Madhubuti foster Africa as locus of identity for Black children and communities.

Akoto and Madhubuti also appear to recognize that some practices that have their roots in Africa must be abandoned and others refined. Madhubuti's assertion clarifies that African people control African culture; African culture does not control African culture. In other words, "We refine and adopt those practices which meet our contemporary needs" (Madhubuti, 1973, p. 44). The Black child is actually an African, and it is the responsibility of African adults to choose from the best that Africans have to offer and move the race forward.

Scholars further the notion that if the Black child is an African, then a sense of responsibility for Africa should be transmitted to him or her. The Afrocentric belief purports that if Blacks in the U.S. understand themselves to be African, such understanding would have a positive impact on their identity development. Knowing who you are is important because it builds self-confidence.

The idea that Blacks are African Americans seems to be rooted in an understanding that Blacks have a unique culture, an African culture, which they brought with them from Africa; however, their experiences in America are unique. The "African American" concept is promoted by Afrocentrics who believe that acknowledging Africa as the root is important but ignoring the fact that those Africans who were forced to come to America have also built a nation takes away from the global accomplishments of African people (Hale-Benson, 1982). Hale-Benson (1982) explained that, "West Africa is the source of many African American Africanisms" (p. 14). Hale-Benson also expressed the fact that certain traditions such as storytelling, weaving, art, craft making, and others have been passed on to African Americans. However, African Americans have developed their own unique expressions of those traditions.

Hales (1997) stated that Afrocentric schools were developed for the purpose of teaching racial identity. While there exists a (small) range between those believing that Blacks are Africans and those believing that Blacks are African Americans, all Afrocentric scholars hold that the Black child must be taught his "Africanness" because if he or she is not, the child will suffer from identity disconnectedness. Earlier Afrocentric writing, such as that of Ridley (1971) and Lomotey (1978), expressed a sentiment of "Black recognition," or the idea that Black people should accept their Blackness and develop camaraderie among one another based on their common struggle in the U.S. The Black Power movement of the 1960s Civil Rights era facilitated the call for identification with Black ideals and a "Black personality."

The calls for Black pride and Black power reflected the sentiment that African Americans must acknowledge their Blackness before their Americanness. However, a more focused call began to develop in the mid-1960s—the call for recognition of Africa as the true source of Black identity—the call for Pan Africanism.

PAN AFRICANISM

Pan Africanism is the belief that all people of African descent are African (Pan African Congress, 1970). Pan Africanism posits that where an individual of African descent currently resides is not applicable to who they are. Malcolm X (1990, 1963) provided a plain-and-simple insight into this idea: ".

.. if a cat delivers babies in an oven, does she deliver biscuits or does she deliver kittens?" (pp. 3-17). The metaphor calls to mind the following: If an African has babies in America, are those babies African or are they Americans? Malcolm X's sentiment mirrors the thinking of Afrocentric educators. Although some Afrocentrics say that he was confusing race with nationality, Malcolm X's overall point about the true racial identity of people of African descent is shared by Afrocentric education leaders such as Madhubuti. Madhubuti and other Afrocentric educationists believe that Afrocentric schools should accept Pan Africanism as the dominant ideology because it brings people of African descent together and concentrates on the common struggles and interests of African people rather than focusing on divisions and differences (Asante, 1980; Brookins, 1984; Doughty, 1973; Hilliard, 1997; Lomotey, 1992; Madhubuti, 1973; Ridley, 1971; Satterwhite, 1971).

Pan Africanist ideology imbues a sense of racial togetherness and pride in children and encourages them to take responsibility for the progress of the African world community. Since most Afrocentric educationists advance Pan Africanism as the dominant ideology, a general Afrocentric approach appears to be favored over a "culturally individualist" approach (Afro-Brazilian, Afro-American, Afro-Jamaican), which these scholars believe concentrates on divisions and differences rather than African roots recognition.

Lomotey (1978) called for the enactment of Pan Africanism by asserting that

> The Pan Africanist principle is the belief that Africa is the home of all people of African descent and all Black people should work for the total liberation and unification of Africa and Africans around the world . . . and schools for African American children should be based upon this principle (p. 36).

45

Afrocentric educationists support the adoption of Pan Africanism because the principle helps to mend some of the fissures that have been caused by the *maafa* (the Middle Passage). It helps to bring people of African descent together to fight against the "dividing and conquering" they have experienced at the hands of outside forces. If the Pan Africanist principle is transmitted to students at an early age, it is hoped that by the time they are adults, they will be socially, politically, and economically productive and help heal a damaged community (Anderson, 2001a).

The rationale supporting Pan Africanist ideology is twofold: firstly, if all people of African descent (worldwide) accept the fact that they are African, the question of identity is resolved—which will lead to greater productivity and psychic resolution of the identity question. Akoto (1992) explained that when a people do not know who they are,

> ...they lack cohesion and are bunched together like so many millions of individual splinters as a consequence of any and all opportunistic currents that move them. In that people's confusion and lack of direction they become the pawns and playthings of those who are directed and powerful (p. 4).

Secondly, Pan Africanist ideology assumes that when the African recognizes that he or she is an African, not African American or Afro-Brazilian, that person accepts responsibility for helping to make Africa better (Cabral, 1070). Akoto and Nkrumah's assertions recall the importance of identifying with an African culture (e.g., Akan) while at the same time holding to cultural practices and understandings (e.g., elder respect and ancestry acknowledgment) for the purpose of not getting splintered off as a consequence of outside opportunism.

Madhubuti (1973) explained that Pan Africanist ideology is not "anti-white" or anti-anything else. The idea is that if children are inculcated with Pan Africanist ideology, they will be functionally educated and will have the necessary tools to ensure the perpetuation of the African race. In the African tradition, "all knowledge is functional . . . it is never knowledge just for knowledge's sake" (Doughty, 1973). In other words, it is never just knowledge for rhetorical regurgitation. Pan Africanism suits the African tradition of advancing functional knowledge because it calls for children of African descent to learn the "3 Rs" but additionally, it imparts a sense of responsibility for the need to change the conditions of African people worldwide. With Africa as the "common theme" among people of African descent, African American culture must be used as a guide to restore African humanity.

AFRICAN AMERICAN CULTURE

Karenga (1966) described culture as the way a people define, create, celebrate, sustain, and develop themselves. Traditionally, the ancestors of people of African descent have used various cultural practices and beliefs as guides to define, create, celebrate, sustain, and develop themselves. Afrocentric educationists purport that this long-standing tradition of using African culture in such ways is threatened because Blacks are unaware of African cultures. According to Asante (1988), because Blacks do not know about their cultures in Africa, " . . .their images, symbols, lifestyles, and manners [become] contradictory and thereby destructive to personal and collective growth and development" (p. 1). According to Asante, such ignorance leads to self-annihilation.

African American children need to be part of an educational system that recognizes their abilities and culture, draws upon these strengths, and incorporates them into the [teaching and] learning process (Baratz and Baratz in Hales, 1997, p. 4). Black educationists believe that knowledge of African/African American cultures is important because without such knowledge, Black children take part in an alien and alienating process of schooling (Hale-Benson, 1982; Lomotey, 1978; Ridley, 1971; Shujaa, 1992). The problem Black children face is that they participate in a process of schooling that is demeaning to them because it does not affirm or recognize Black contributions to world progress (Hales, 1997). If culture is the way a people define, create, celebrate, sustain, and develop themselves, Black children are in trouble because the public education system does not teach them about the significance of their historical journey or the struggles and accomplishments that Black people have made. Lomotey (1978) explained that

> Information about African people is usually left out of textbooks, and when it is included, it usually starts discussing slavery, and leaves out any information that can help Black children gain a sense of responsibility and respect for self . . . (p. 25).

Some Afrocentric scholars believe that Blacks ". . . have a fundamentally African worldview" (Ridley, 1971, p. 19). This belief is supported by recognition that certain Black "traits" had their roots in Africa, such as certain relational thinking and rhythmic propensities (Hale-Benson, 1982). In Hale-Benson's (1982) study of Black children and their cultural frameworks, she explained, "West Africa is the source of many African American Africanisms" (p. 14). The idea is that those who have contact with Black children should possess functional knowledge about Africa because African cultures are at the root of who Black children really are. This belief challenges the sentiment that Blacks are "American" and have existed in the U.S. for so long that they have lost touch with their African roots.

Some Afrocentric educationists appear to focus more on the political aspects of Black children gaining knowledge of their history. Lomotey (1992) suggested,

> African centered education seeks to meet a set of cultural
> as well as academic and social goals . . . [Educators] must
> identify culturally with African American children to
> teach them about their culture, life, and about where they
> fit in society and the world (p. 457).

Functional knowledge of African/African American
cultures transmits a sense of "location" for the Black child.
Asante (1999) explained that Afrocentric education puts the
Black child in a "centered place." The centered location (i.e.,
Africa), anchors and roots the Black child so that he or she
is not ideologically "floating around," thinking he or she is
someone he or she is not. Proper cultural grounding places
the child in context, which is necessary because the dominant
Eurocentric/American culture has created mayhem for
Blacks because children are expected to behave in ways that
are not consistent with who they are.

Hale-Benson (1982) detailed, "There are important
cultural differences between Europeans and Africans that
account for the different learning styles of African American
children" (p. xiii). Lee (1992) suggested that when African/
African American culture is used as a means for educating
Black children, research shows that they flourish. Afrocentric
educationists believe that the American public school system
is designed to maintain the status quo and does not transmit
a sense of African agency (Brookins, 1984; Hilliard, 1997;
Lomotey, 1978).

Still another Afrocentric scholar explained that one
of the reasons Blacks have such a difficult time in the
American public education system is the mismatch between
the cultural viewpoints of Blacks and the culture of the
schools they attend (Hales, 1997). Afrocentrics hold that the
"achievement gap" is merely a result of the larger problem
of societal racism and discrimination, and the schools are
not equipped with the right resources to teach Black children.
Tharp and Gallimore (1991) reported ". . . research indicates

that children's identity, culture, and social experiences are foundations for academic success" (p. 28). The authors suggest that if African/African American cultural knowledge is not part of the educational enterprise, then Black children will surely fail to reach the higher goal of African agency. Lomotey (1992) posited that "children learn best in an environment in which their own culture is the focus of the curriculum" (p. 461). Writers seem to attach more importance to African cultural knowledge in general (i.e., finding common African cultural themes) than advancing a specific culture that people of African descent should choose.

There is an overarching suggestion that Black children are doomed from the outset in American public schools because teachers are not equipped with knowledge of African/African American cultural frameworks. Although she is not an Afrocentric educationist, Lisa Delpit (2001) explained that no one knows the best methods for teaching Black children because no one really has been taught who they are. The literature draws a picture of a school where European American children and European American teachers are the majority, yet no one knows the best practices for teaching or reaching European American children either. Afrocentric educationists call for a sojourn of the insidiousness of ignorance of methods and cultures, and they call for a re-conceptualization of Black education in order to help Black students to become productive members of society (Akoto, 2001; Anderson, 2001a; Armah, 1979; Asante, 1991; Hale-Benson, 1982; Kunjufu, 1995; Wilson, 1993).

As stated previously, Afrocentric education is not simply concerned with teaching the "3 Rs"; rather, it is the necessary educational method to use for a complete and total change in the education of Black children. African cultural infusion is important for Black children because the culture carries within it certain values that have been used to guide the actions of people of African descent throughout time. Afrocentric educationists stress the importance of an African-centered value system for Black children.

Literature

African Values Adoption and Transmission

African cultures carry within them values and spiritual systems. For example, Akoto explained that, "religion was unnecessary in African culture when it was practiced before the European invasion, because the cultures already had within them the necessary spiritual and values systems needed for our commune and survival" (K. A. Akoto, personal communication, 2002). The Nguzo Saba of Njia is a good example of a general Afrocentric value system used by Afrocentric educationists. For example, Kwame Akoto uses Nguzo Saba in his African-centered school; however, the Nguzo Saba system is not part of the Akan system that Baba San uses in his own personal life practice.

"Nguzo Saba" is a Kiswahili word that means, "Seven Principles of a Black value system." Maulana Karenga (1966) developed the Nguzo Saba as the cornerstone principles of his system of Njia/Kawaida (The Way). Karenga's research included studying several cultural groups on the continent of Africa as he attempted to find ways to demonstrate what an African system is, and how such value systems relate to the cultures of Black people. Afrocentric educationists believe that Black children need to know the values that have helped sustain the Black community.

The Seven Principles and their popularly used Kiswahili translations as Karenga (1966) noted are: 1) Umoja (unity); 2) Kujichagulia (self-determination); 3) Ujima (collective work and responsibility); 4) Ujamaa (cooperative economics); 5) Nia (purpose); 6) Kuumba (creativity); and (7) Imani (faith).

The Nguzo Saba is a frame of reference for Afrocentric educationists. Madhubuti (1973) stated that, "Our frame of reference has been reversed from that of our African selves to accepting a frame of reference based upon the value system of Europeans and European Americans" (p. 25). Afrocentrics charged that ". . . the educational

51

experiences occurring in schools today tend to be conforming with the dispositions and experiences of European American middle-class children, for example, a focus on dominant cultural values. . ." (Hales, 1997, p. 190). African value systems serve to recapture the essence of "who African people really are" and reinstate values and principles they used in the past to secure their future. Hilliard (1997) stated that "...in order for African Americans to resurrect themselves, old traditions and values must be used" (p. 69).

Lomotey (1992) interjected: "African-centered education engenders a reorientation of students' values and actions" (p. 456). Afrocentric educationists believe that Blacks are not acting in their own best interest because they have adopted an alien value system. The Nguzo Saba and other value systems (e.g., the value systems within African cultures) center on values that will help to uplift the Black community. Brandwein (1981) explained:

> Education [is] the process of transmitting from one generation to the next, knowledge of the values . . . and all the things that give a particular cultural orientation its uniqueness. Every cultural group must provide from this transmission or it will cease to exist (p. 3).

Afrocentric educationists are concerned that Blacks have adopted a frivolous value system for two reasons: (a) their meager positions in American society, and (b) their reactions to and relationships with the system of capitalism. A reorientation of the Black value system that calls on tradition and culture is critical because if something is not done about the "inappropriate behavior patterns" (Anderson, 2001a) of African Americans, they face annihilation (Shujaa, 1993).

The rationale behind using the Nguzo Saba and other African value systems seems to be that this inculcation of relevant values will lead to a commitment to the principles and practices of togetherness and collective action. The Nguzo Saba calls for Blacks to build and maintain the communities of which they are a part. Madhubuti (1973) detailed that "Our survival lies in our ability to operate out of an African frame of reference based upon a proven value system that incorporates a sense of African love and responsibility" (p. 14). This type of transmission leads to a sense of African nationalism.

Black Nationalism

Afrocentric scholars ask: What space can Blacks call their own? In the U.S. there are many areas that are designated for certain people, for example, in New York, Chicago, Los Angeles, Washington, DC, and several cities in Washington state, there are places called "China Towns." These towns within cities are comprised mostly of Asians from China who live in a shared space, own the shops, stores, and schools in those areas, and support each other's endeavors. In Miami, Florida, and cities in such states as California, Arizona, and New Mexico, Latinos have similar communities. Also, in New York, Cincinnati, Chicago, and many other cities in the U.S., there are many Jewish communities. While Blacks (just as others) live relatively segregated lives (Iceland & Weinberg, 2000), the question is: "Why do they not own and control the areas where they live" (Anderson, 2001b; Kunjufu, 2002)?

Afrocentric education scholar Jawanza Kunjufu's (2002) book *Black Economics* explores the baffling phenomenon of Blacks, living relatively segregated lives, who do not own the shops, stores, businesses, and schools in their neighborhoods. In the past, when others (such as political leaders) asked why this phenomenon of destitute communities exists, the question has not been framed in an educational sense. However, Kunjufu explained that in order for Blacks to take control over their lives, they must be taught how to do so. That is, the only way that Blacks will be able to "take control of the psychic and physical space that they call theirs, and [to take agency] over their lives and the institutions needed for their survival" (Akoto, 1992, p. 3) is to be educated to do so.

Black children must be the catalysts for helping to instill a sense of agency in the Black community because generations of Blacks have only been taught how to consume and be dependent on outside entities (Anderson, 2001a). Agency eventually leads toward nation-building. Agency and nation-building involve the intentional and focused attempt to "develop African youth to be specifically trained to further develop and administrate the state" (Lomotey, 1978, p. 5). Blacks cannot learn to "administrate the state" if they are not equipped with attitudes that teach them that they, in fact, should administer their communities and be agents to uplift the Black race.

Black nationalism is the carrier of such sentiment because it teaches Black children that Blacks constitute a nation (Akoto, 1992). This belief, coupled with the belief that Blacks should liberate and build the psychic space that they call theirs, revolutionizes the current attitude that permeates Black communities. Lomotey (1978) explained that ". . . the American educational system will never meet the needs of African American students because the successful accomplishment of that end is not in the best interest of those who are in power" (p. 11). Carter G. Woodson (1933) suggested that the education that Blacks receive only teaches them to serve in the system that oppresses them; therefore, they participate in their own oppression.

The preceding are a very strong yet simple claims to understand to consider the principles of capitalism.

Afrocentric educationists are charged with transitioning Black children from the "world's puppets and playthings" (Akoto, 1992) to "thinkers" who are able to build a nation (Akoto, 1992; Asante, 1999; Brookins, 1984; Doughty, 1973; Hilliard, 1997; Lomotey, 1978; Ridley, 1971).

Anderson (2001b) explained that Blacks are the number one consumers in the world:

> As a group, last year [they] spent over $800 billion. A dollar turns over once in the Black community; it turns over six times in the white community, five times in the Asian community, and seven times in the Jewish community (p. 44).

Afrocentric education scholars purport that the principles and practices of Black nationalism will transmit a sense of agency to Black children and thereby to Black communities. The American public education system is not preparing Blacks to be producers and controllers of their own destinies. Afrocentric educationists call for Blacks to be equipped with the tools they need to bring themselves out of the "spending cults" they are in and into a world of productive activity.

Black nationalism is a radical concept when compared to the present order. But, when viewed through the lens of Afrocentric self-preservation, it is not so politically charged. Furthermore, nationalistic behavior parallels that of other groups in society who live in relatively segregated areas (U.S. Census, 2000) and build and maintain institutions to perpetuate themselves and their culture (Asante, 1998). In order for Black nationalism to work, and in order for a sense of agency to be transmitted to people of African descent, Black people must be properly organized and prepared to take on such responsibility (Akoto, 1992). The literature identifies nationalistic community building as a call for Blacks to build institutions that will sustain African life.

COMMUNITY CONTROL AND INSTITUTION BUILDING

Community control involves making important decisions about the institutions that exist in one's community. Institution building involves creating the necessary agencies that are designed to "impart knowledge, skills, values,, and attitudes necessary to survive and progress" (Doughty, 1973, p. 3). Independent Black institutions (IBIs) were designed for the purpose of creating the necessary agencies to serve the interests of the Black community. According to Doughty (1973), ". . . the belief can be maintained that the masses of Black children will show significantly higher achievement rates in separate, independent, Black schools, not in desegregated or integrated schools" (p. 111). Doughty claims that power, ideology, relevant curriculum, and sound instructional practices are important concepts that are properly transmitted in IBIs. Lomotey (1978) pointed out that there is some evidence that suggests that Black children in IBIs perform above the norm, and Ratteray (1990) found that Blacks in IBIs score higher on standardized achievement tests. These findings, among other observations and perceived cultural needs, lead Afrocentric educationists to believe that it is optimal for Blacks to attend IBIs.

The assumption made by Afrocentric educationists seems to be that Black-owned and controlled educational systems ". . . will eliminate the injustices and miseducation of the present educational system, and create a strong basis for change in the lives of people of African descent" (Doughty, 1973, p. 3). Afrocentric educationists do not believe that education should be solely for personal gain. The goal is to change the entire community, but in order to do so, Afrocentric scholars desire a generation of Africans that are taught from a perspective that is "self-centered." (A "community" self). Lomotey (1978) explained that "[IBIs] are vehicles for community development. . . " (p. 35).

Literature

Lomotey and others (such as Asante, 1990; Akoto, 1992, 1999; and Kambon, 1992) believe that if Black children are imbued with a sense of agency, which includes owning and controlling all of the institutions in one's community, they will eventually take control of their own destiny—which adheres to the principle of *kujichagulia* (self-determination). The rationale behind the imperatives of community control and institution building is most simply stated by Madhubuti (1973): "Either a people prepare their youth to be responsible and responsive to their own needs, or someone else will—for their needs" (p. 30). Afrocentric educationists believe that Black children should be taught to take control of their communities because the current arrangement is dehumanizing, demoralizing, and leads to low self-esteem. The idea is that self-made and self-controlled institutions are more likely to produce self-interested results. For example, Lomotey (1978) has summed up the idea by explaining that

> . . . the American educational system will never meet the needs of Black students because the successful accomplishment of that end is not in the best interest of those who are in power. What we are suggesting then is that public education in the U.S. has not worked in the best interest of African American people. Some of us have consequently concluded that an alternative (the IBI) needs to be developed in order to address the specific needs of African American children (p. 11).

As stated earlier, the ability to control the institutions in one's community is tantamount to having control over one's own destiny. Afrocentrics hold that if someone else builds and controls the institutions in the Black community, then Blacks are at the whims of those who control those institutions (Asante, 1980, 1999; Hilliard, 1997; Lomotey, 1978, 1992; Madhubuti, 1973). Afrocentric education appears to be a fairly simple call for Africans to be taught to control their own lives. It follows that since the adults in Black communities have been miseducated (Woodson, 1933), a process of reclaiming responsibility and resurrecting the race must take place in schools for generations to come. Afrocentric educators worry that although schools train, they do not educate.

THE CALL FOR EDUCATION, NOT SCHOOLING/TRAINING

In his book, Shujaa (1994) skillfully explained the difference between education and schooling while also highlighting the detrimental effects when one is mistaken for the other:

> The schooling process is designed to provide an ample supply of people who are loyal to the nation-state and who have learned the skills needed to perform the work that is necessary to maintain the dominance of the European-American elite in its social order. For African Americans, individual success in schooling is often simply a matter of demonstrating one's ability to represent the interests of the European American elite. Through such a process, African people as a group are able to derive little benefit from the schooling of our members and, even then, it is most likely to be in the interests of the European American elite for us to do so (Shujaa, 1994, p. 10).

Shujaa's stance elaborated on Woodson's (1933) assertion that ". . . [African Americans] have an attitude of contempt toward their own people because in their own as well as their mixed schools, they are taught to admire the Hebrew, Greek, and Latin and taught to despise the African" (p. 1). This behavior explains why Afrocentric educationists believe that Blacks must have an African-centered education. Hilliard (1997) further explained that schooling does not transform individuals. He stated, ". . . we can expect little more than schooling from America's public institutions; we cannot expect education for our transformation" (p. 7).

The purpose of schooling is to maintain the status quo (Lomotey, 1978). Obviously, Afrocentric educationists are unhappy with the status of Blacks, so they call for true education of Black children. Lomotey (1992) further explained that capitalism makes it necessary for Blacks to continue to be miseducated.

The goals of Afrocentric education do not seem possible unless Blacks begin to receive true education, which is primarily "knowledge of self" (Akbar, 1992). Knowledge of self is inclusive of information pertaining to one's personal identity, group identity (Pan Africanist), cultural identity and recognition, appropriate and proper values, a national plan/agenda for betterment, and the building of institutions to perpetuate "self." According to Lomotey (1992), it is improbable that the education Blacks receive in public institutions will ever reform itself to the point where Blacks receive the tools that are necessary for them to have agency over their lives. For this reason, Afrocentric educationists call for a revolutionary re-conceptualization of Black education.

IMPLICATIONS OF CULTURAL-REATTACHMENT AFROCENTRIC EDUCATION

Cultural-reattachment Afrocentric education suggests that Blacks must re-think what it means to be educated and successful. By way of clarification, as in Shujaa (1993), Afrocentric educationists imply that the Black community progresses when a type of thinking prevails that requires one's educational attainment to be measured by the use of such education to effect change in the community. Therefore, degrees in computer science and economics are not valued by their being acquired, but instead by the acquirer's commitment to use knowledge gained to spawn progress, change, and cultural reattachment in Black communities. The imperatives of Afrocentric education beseech adherents toward progress and cultural application in all arenas of life, which enhances Black community life as opposed to individual "success." Enhancements on this level generate authentic community racial/cultural power.

Adults (e.g., parents, community leaders) in the Black community are able to foster a process of cultural reattachment for youth only when they themselves become familiar with the conceptual tools of reattachment. For this reason, many Afrocentric education scholars host regular community forums that are designed to enhance the community's understanding of the concepts they espouse. Even though the imperatives of Afrocentric education are unpopular in the mainstream educational offering, it is important for parents and other stakeholders to support the work of Afrocentric educationists as they work to reattach the community to the culture(s) that may have enough healing power to reach out to the community. This may very well be what is needed to educate children of African descent and address their problems.

The literature produced by Afrocentric educationists argues that in order to improve educational outcomes for Black children, attention must first be paid to the overall social problems within the Black community. Cultural-reattachment Afrocentric educationists have clarified their stance that focusing on the contemporary education issues alone (e.g., Black children's low math and reading scores and/or the achievement gap) is at best a "quick fix" to a problem and does not address the field of education at all. However, teachers who are familiar with the cultural imperatives of Afrocentric education (as discussed in this book) are armed with some necessary tools that they can use to better serve Black children.

Literature

Afrocentric educationists' cultural imperatives are basic: know one's cultural history, practice one's culture, and have a sense of connectedness to the people in one's cultural group. However, they have also made it clear that because of the Black community's lack of power and historically low placement in the American social order, achieving such basic requisites (e.g., affording Black children and communities knowledge of African value systems) becomes a very political issue.

Since many people are unaware of what Afrocentric education really is (Akoto, 1992; Hilliard, 1997; Lee, 1992), it is obvious that knowledge of the cultural imperatives is a first step toward understanding. It is crucial to note that the cultural imperatives do not represent the full make-up of cultural-reattachment Afrocentric education. Instead, they represent the necessary initial requirement of being able to understand the thinking behind the theory and the ability to place definitions on commonly used words.

Having definitions and explanations of the words and ideas used by African-centered educationists is critical. However, equally crucial is the fact that many cultural-reattachment Afrocentric educationists have translated these concepts into practical use within their communities. Examples of different indigenous groups that have provided guidance for cultural reattachment include the Kmt, Yoruba, and Akan groups from Africa.

The Akan Example: Learning African Culture for the Purpose of Re-Africanization

Cultural-reattachment Afrocentric education is not simply a theoretical postulate with no practical utility. Many Africans from around the world are literally reattaching themselves and their families to indigenous African cultural practices. As stated before, some people of African descent are reattaching to cultures such as ancient Kmt culture (Kmt/

61

Nubia/Egypt), Yoruba (Nigeria), and Akan (Ghana). The similarities among these cultural groups are more evident than their differences. I recently visited a Yoruba village in Nigeria and an Akan village in Ghana. In this chapter I recount some of my experiences among the Akan people of Ghana. My experience with Blacks born in the U.S. who are *reattaching* to Akan culture was striking because it runs very much parallel to the practices I saw among the indigenous practitioners of Akan in Ghana.

Akin to most African cultural groups, traditional Akan cosmology includes conceptions of a Divine One (God, *Nyame*). This finding runs contrary to westernized notions that Africans are "pagan" and/or "polytheistic." The evidence is overwhelming that the conception of "one God" comes from Africa. This is important to note because many Blacks (especially African American Christians and Muslims) fear re-becoming African because they have been taught that Africans are pagans or believe in many gods. The fear of such things is both unfounded and unnecessary.

The Akan also believe that those people who came before but are no longer living (ancestors, *nsamanfoo*) should be acknowledged and remembered for the things they did that have made it possible for the current generation to be alive now. I found some villages where traditional cultural practices still exist en masse (comparatively speaking), some where such practices moderately exist, and some where such practices hardly exist at all in Ghana.

I visited the "Ago" village where tradition exists en masse. I found that the Akan do not value "religion," yet every aspect of their lives is overwhelmingly spiritual. It is important to note that there is a vast difference between indigenous Akan practice and current practice. Current practice has been negatively influenced by outsiders such as the British. However, there *are* places where such influence has been minimal. One such example is Ago village.

LITERATURE

While in Ago I recall having had difficulty understanding what was going on around me until I encountered a woman named Hora, whom I met at a shrine (temple, *Abosom fie*). One of the things I was perplexed about was all of the symbolism in the dancing. I thought the dancing was for celebratory purposes, but Hora explained to me very patiently that, "The *hyere* [white blessing powder] keeps the white and the red sacred. My hand motion is like that because I am my grandfather now. I am not myself." Keeping red and black sacred refers to keeping "elements" separate (e.g., keeping wind and rain separate).

Perplexed, I continued to ask questions of Hora and her husband, Kwase, about the nature of "the dancer not being herself, but instead being her grandfather." For instance, while dancing and spreading the hyere, the dancer began smoking a cigarette and talking to onlookers in a man's voice (literally) about the harms of jet engine fuel. It was not the dancer at all but, again, her grandfather.

Akan ethos is primarily spiritual. Whereas in the West one can live a secular life, among the Akan the cultural life is spiritual in itself, and that which is observable and touchable is not valued over that which is not observable or touchable. Also, community life is a spiritual activity that is about togetherness.

For example, Hora invited me to their home for dinner after we left the shrine. As we left the shrine with the other participants, someone called out "*Asante Kotoko*" (Ashantis with the porcupine totem). That led to the response "*wokum apem a apem beba*" (kill thousands of us and thousands will come back!). Hora explained to me that they were chanting what was originally a war chant. In the same way that a porcupine's quills grow back if you cut them, if you take out one thousand Akan people, one thousand will come back. Songs and chants that express important aspects of mundane cultural life and important beliefs within Akan society are commonplace, and they occur frequently

63

throughout the day. The people sing and chant to keep focused on work, build harmony and togetherness, and enjoy the work that they must complete.

Before we reached Hora and Kwase's home, Kwase ran ahead and I saw him go quickly into the house. When Hora and I reached the house, I noticed several children and elders sitting around a table; on it were rice and fish in a large bowl. There were several young adults there as well who stood in back of the elders and children. I was greeted by every member of the family with a handshake and an introduction. Hora offered bits of information about each of the family members. Hora's 92-year-old mother said some things to me in Twi, a language I did not understand. Hora said, "She is offering your blessings to God and to the ancestors for making it here safely and praying for your safe return back to the U.S."

I was asked if I had something to say to them. A bit overwhelmed at being formally greeted into a home where they had no prior knowledge I was coming (except for Kwase's mere five-minute warning), I thanked them for opening their home to me and for being so welcoming. Even though many of them spoke English, Hora translated my words into Twi. I looked at their faces after the translation and was surprised. My eyes were fixed on Mama Tima (Hora's mother). She nodded her head "yes" slowly, with her arms crossed, her wrinkled eyes a bit squinted, and a frowned brow; there was a bit of silence and she seemed to be "hunting" for a smile. I was curious and became self-conscious. The room seemed to be waiting for Mama Tima. Finally, several seconds later, she waved her hand over food and smiled, and then the young adults prepared plates and utensils for everyone. One of the young adults made plates for Mama Tima, Hora, and Kwase. It was the "fourth night" so the stool was cleaned and a plate of rice was put aside for the *nsamanfoo*. Different shrines have different nights when they perform certain rituals such as cleaning stools and/or placing food aside for the nsamanfoo. Questions ran through my mind because of Mama Tima's silence and slow head nod after my greeting. It was not a negative response, but it seemed like she was "concerned."

During dinner I asked Hora about Mama Tima's response, and she reassured me that all was well. I was not satisfied. I asked her what she thought of my response and she said, "Why do you put yourself to worry about it?" Finally, after much prodding it was explained, "You thanked us for welcoming you and feeding you, but you made no other acknowledgements."

I found out that in a way they expected me to acknowledge God and/or the ancestors in some way. Praying and giving thanks are different in Akan context than in Western context in that in the West one can simply express thanks that a thing happened or did not happen. But in Akan context, a person "acknowledges God and/or venerates the ancestors for their help in making a thing happen or not happen." There is just as much knowledge of (i.e., belief in) things that are seen as there is in the unseen.

Certainly Western institutions such as Christianity make spiritual acknowledgement, but in indigenous African practice all aspects of cultural life intersperse with spirituality in such ways that there is no disconnection. There is no such thing as "the secular." Living is holistically spiritual.

Kwadwo, a very astute young male adult member of the family who lived in the West for three years but was now home in the village permanently, said to me so eloquently, "What you may see as religious life is a communal affair woven into our culture." I understood. It also began to make sense to me as one reason why Blacks in the U.S. may be experiencing difficulty. If for centuries Africans lived in communities where spiritual and communal life were one but now (in the American context) live where spiritual "behavior" is only appropriate in certain settings, as psychologist Na'im Akbar explains, they could be experiencing "cultural schizophrenia." It is quite possible that a more seamless African spiritual environment could help Blacks. Consistency between home, school, and spiritual life is a major push within African-centered schools. The way the people behave with one another in the indigenous African settings that I visited generates an environment of togetherness and belonging. Feeling connected with a sense of purpose creates a sense of unity (that they are all in accord with common purposes) within Akan society. There is a seamlessness that exists from family life to the shrine to interactions between members of the community to how they see people who are not Akan. While such practices and understandings may be foreign to Western tastes and preferences, such behavior and beliefs make children feel secure and could be of great use to Black children in the U.S. But re-Africanization is necessary. Attempting to adopt certain cultural behaviors without re-Africanizing will do no good.

AKAN IDENTITY

The Akan have a proverb, "*Asem a ehia Akanfoo no na Ntafoo de goro brekete*," which means, "A matter that troubles the Akan people, the people of Gonja take to play the brekete drum." After some de-coding, this is found to be a proverb that is used to tease the Dagomba people of the northern region, to make them feel how important the Akans are. The ability to identify with others who are also part of the same group is very important to Africans. Even many of the less traditional (i.e., westernized) Ghanaians are still very proud to belong to their cultural group. More westernized Ghanaians who identify themselves as Akan revealed surprisingly strong feelings of pride toward the Akan cultural traditions even when the person acknowledges him/herself as being westernized and/or when the person verbalizes little to no disdain toward the philosophy and processes of westernization. Even though the major metropolises of Ghana have become virtually completely westernized (via colonization and neo-colonization), traditional African ethos has not been totally erased. For example, Christianity is not indigenous to the Akan, yet many who describe themselves as Christians report that at times they revert to Akan (traditional) cultural ways when necessary. To illustrate, Akosua, a 34-year-old woman who self-identifies as being both Christian and Akan, provides some revelations: "I am Christian, but I pray and pray for healing and when I cannot get healing for me or my children or for my family I go to [the] village and I ask the Okomfo [Akan traditional priest] for what I need ... and it works."

Surprisingly, many of the other Christians follow the same pattern—they revert to African traditional healing practices when the feel the need to do so. What is most surprising about the fact that they engage in such reverting is that they are in direct conflict with Christian beliefs and they know it! Akosua explained, "When I go to [the] village they may call upon ancestors, Nyame, and they have spiritual chants and maybe dances to ward off the spirit that is causing the problem, but at church they say that it is not right. They say that it is backward."

She continued, "I don't know. Maybe it is not so evil because we do chanting in the church ... and [get] the remedies from the village." She paused, "...they work." She then shocked me by saying, "Many of the white priests come to the village for traditional healing too!" I could not get her or anyone else to elaborate on that: White Christian leaders visiting traditional African shrines on the down low, then telling African Americans that traditional African shrine practices amount to paganism and will get them sent to hell. This oddity must be further investigated.

Regardless of the degree to which the Ghanaian may or may not revert to traditional ways, they are proud about their unique cultural heritage. Ghanaians use their traditional culture as the first referent for their interactions with other people. For example, many Akans primarily refer to their traditional culture to guide their interactions and operations with family, community members, and elders. Kwadwo clarifies that Akan "is the first comprehensive value system that I use to interact with people." For example, they are socialized from childhood toward the traditional practice of greeting everyone except elders by asking them how they are doing, "*Ete sen?*" Children are taught about the importance of communal unity via commonly used folk songs, for example:

Praye wo ho ye	The broom as it exists
wo yi baako	When you take one stick
a na ebu	Then it breaks
woka bo mu a	When you put it together
emmbu	It will not break

Communal unity is very important, but the most important aspect of that unity is respect for elders. Older people are not asked "*Ete sen?*" Instead, it is "*Ma/Da mi pawochaw ete sen?*" Of course, *ma* is feminine and *da* is masculine. Elders are to be greeted when seen. Elders also have wisdom that they may share if the younger person is appropriately respectful. Kwadwo explains,

> It's common for kids walking home from school to greet "good afternoon" (*ma aha*) or "good evening" (*ma adwo*) when they see an older man or woman walking past them. This is one indication of how younger people in the Akan society are constantly encouraged to show reverence to older ones.
> Older people (*mpanyinfo*) are wise and have experienced things beyond what younger people may have experienced. As a result, younger people ought to respect the older ones because they could teach them what they have learned

LITERATURE

about life if the younger ones are humble enough. Some
may argue that this aspect of the culture makes children
fearful and can lead to wrong indoctrinations. That may
be the case, but an older person who is generally considered
injudicious (*sansanyi*), is so labeled and children are not
penalized for disregarding his or her opinions.

When a female younger person greets an older person,
she places her hands midriff with palms up, slightly bows,
and offers the greeting. Males who are younger "salute" the
older person and offer the greeting.

Akan culture is family oriented and makes people
feel a sense of belonging. While at Mama Tima's family
house, extended members of the family visited
(unannounced) and were hugged, hands were shook, food
was offered, and the visitors were encouraged to sit down
and get comfortable. Hora explained to me that Akans share
a deep belief that family unity is of great importance, that it
is a system of networks that enhances one's social capital.
The system of networks enhances social capital because one
calls upon family to help meet one's needs and wants, and
through such calling, the utilized networks become stronger
and the links to other extended members are compounded.

Kwadwo explained that, "The concept of family is
not restricted to the nuclear family but also the extended
family that may include uncles, aunts, first cousins, second
cousins, in-laws, and the like who are always there to help."
While Africans are often seen by the West as being
technologically unsophisticated, their family and social
networks are awe-inspiring.

Akan cultural philosophy creates an atmosphere
wherein young people are clear on the gender roles. Girls
are reared toward being very nurturing. Kwadwo explained,
"When my dad would come home, my sister would ask him
if he needed anything to eat. I would ask if he wanted me to
help paint or something."

69

While under any circumstances (Western liberty or Akan essentialist) cases of abuse can occur, the unambiguous roles in Akan society clarify for children their future responsibilities as husbands and wives. In fact, the children are reared from an early age toward becoming good husbands and wives. In that same vain, children are taught that they are representatives of their families and that any bad things they might do will spoil the family name. Kwadwo enlightened me on the extreme importance of family name:

> When you meet someone and you ask them for their name, they might say their first name, so then you ask them for their last name so that you will know what clan or family group they come from. Once you know that, you can associate them with things about that clan. When you are a child, your parents always say to you, do not do anything that will mess up our name—and they are very serious about it!

African cultural groups are proud of their family name and fight to protect it. In the U.S., Blacks have names that do not represent their family lineage. Instead, Blacks have names that represent a European legacy. African-centered schools encourage children and families to adopt African names so that they can pick up the African legacy and break the cycle that was began by European invaders. However, re-Africanization is not possible by simply taking on an African name. Through a spiritual process, one must change his/her way of "being in the world" to match African culturo-cosmological ways of knowing.

African cultural practices and traditions may serve as a potential corrective to the myriad problems faced by Black people in the U.S. because those practices and traditions encourage togetherness and a sense of connectedness. Psychologists such as Na'im Akbar, Asa Hilliard, and Wade Nobles have all confirmed that children of African descent need to feel that sense of connectedness in order to be truly productive and happy. African-centered educationists attempt to bring about this sense of connectedness and community by emphasizing the importance of one's cultural identity. While groups such as African Americans are being turned off to Africa because it has been stigmatized as being a backward, unsophisticated place, deep within the indigenous structures of African groups are powerful tools that can be used to resurrect people of African descent as well as help to provide guidance to the entire world.

AFRICAN HUMANISM AND COMMUNITY

From a Western perspective, the aesthetic environment in Africa and even among the Akan people leaves much to be desired. The roads need work, sewer systems need to be updated (and sometimes installed), the dust and exhaust from automobiles in the cities is overwhelming, and much of the infrastructure is outdated. However, after spending time with the people, it becomes apparent why their societies have lasted so long. In the case of the Akans, the main reason is that Akan culture is very humanistic. The values inherent in the culture speak to the sense of peace and harmony within the society. People are meaningfully engaged in the daily lives of one another, and respect for elders is critical. Family is one's primary responsibility, and the social connections between people are primarily functions of families coming together for some purpose, such as farming.

Children are reared to understand that they represent their families and are taught gender roles and responsibilities from a very young age. Hora explained that her grandmother taught her from age three that "...a good wife knows how her husband is feeling even without him telling her." In the West we are trained to wonder what, if anything, the husband knows about his wife. Akan culture answers such questions without them ever being asked.

Perhaps the most striking aspect of my study of Akan culture is the fact that by Western economic standards most of the Akan are poverty-stricken—while at the same time their lives are rich beyond measure. It is fair to say that having one's basic needs met requires much harder work in Africa than in the West, but it is also fair to say that their lives are complete with family and supportive communities that make group members feel a sense of communal affection and belonging. People are genuinely happy simply being together. There is less crime, there is no epidemic of Black men and women being imprisoned, Black men are more often present for their families, there are clear roles for men and women (although in the West this is not valued, according to Africans, it works well for them), and as a rule children are cared for and elders are respected.

Even the above very small excerpt from field notes of my findings indicates that the Black community can benefit a great deal from adopting the principles and practices of African culture because the communal sentiment under indigenous practice is, for the most part, non-violent. People are not suspicious of one another, and there are unspoken but agreed upon cultural ways of behavior. Even though the environment in the U.S. is more materially luxurious, the conditions within Black communities in the U.S. are often violent, and Blacks are more suspicious of one another now than they have ever been.

African-centered education is a holistic endeavor that calls for people of African descent to re-Africanize and stop allowing Black children to be the playthings of researchers in the U.S. and Europe.

WHAT EDUCATORS MUST KNOW: AN AFRICAN HISTORICAL STORY

Literature

Even though much information is available pertaining to history education, educators still find themselves in a quandary as to *exactly* what to teach Black children. History books may be plentiful, but the standardized requirements of school districts are uncompromising. It should be the responsibility of educators to decide exactly what they are going to teach in their classrooms, and when classroom doors are closed, we must trust that teachers are going to do their very best job of reaching their charges. Instead of offering another dreadful list of requirements for educators, following are some important moments in African history that represent transition points for Africans. These transition points and important African historical accomplishments are presented chronologically later in this book.

If educators of African children (and really all children) take the time to understand the historical story presented here (for little Darnell's sake, which will be explained later!), not as the complete African story (which would take 3.2 million years to tell!), but instead as an important outline for beginning to understand African history, education for Black children will improve. The outline that is provided in this book is doable even in the face of the uncompromising standardized requirements. This means that teachers can use this timeline as a starting point for their own effort to re-Africanize and then reach out to others with the information they learn here.

The first part of the book has set the stage for understanding the importance of re-Africanization. The second part will demonstrate the critical importance of understanding that Black children do, indeed, respond to knowledge that pertains to them. Follow this story and use it as an example of how we must work with our children and sacrifice the most Eurocentric parts of ourselves.

The goal of telling this story is to offer another tool in the arsenal of information on exactly *who* the African child is. The following should encourage educators and caretakers of African children to get excited about African history and culture. Use this resource as a starting point in your attempt to reattach African children to African culture. Share this resource with others in your community!

CHAPTER 4: An Important African Story

Getting to Know Darnell, Culturally

I met a boy named Darnell Lumpkin who asked me to tell as many teachers as possible this story.

Darnell Lumpkin was always in the principal's office for something! He was there for talking, couldn't stay in his seat, disrupting the teachers when they were trying to teach, messing with other students, and couldn't keep his hands to himself. The teacher would ask a question, and he'd just yell out the answer. It never failed that on any given day, to the principal's office Darnell would somehow find his way. Whether at the beginning, the middle, or at day's end, Darnell had a spot he'd always be in: right across from the secretary, sitting in a chair.

Darnell had been there so many times he was no longer scared of the principal. It got to the point where he knew how the secretary answered the phones. "Thank you for calling Ida Elementary; one moment; could you please hold on?" They had called his mom so many times to talk to her about her child, that the secretary put her numbers on the office phone speed dial: Numbers 2, 3, 4—and Darnell knew that too. He'd just wait to see which number Mrs. Jenkins would press to see if she'd get through.

"Press number 4, Mrs. Jenkins, my mom's out of the office today."

"Darnell, how'd you know that?" Mrs. Jenkins would say.

"She told me this morning when I left the house that if you were going to call, to tell you she'd be out."

This whole situation was really pretty sad, but what was worse was that Darnell was missing class. He was missing out on math, on gym, and music too, writing and language arts, and most importantly his reading group.

Spending so much time in the principal's office, Darnell Lumpkin was falling behind.

Let us fast forward to 10 years later. Darnell is now 18 but his knowledge is not much greater. Darnell was pushed through every single grade because no one wanted to keep him for a second year, would you? Teacher after teacher knew that he was coming, and they'd get into debates over who was going to take that Darnell Lumpkin.

As Darnell Lumpkin aged, so did his devious ways. Now he'd gotten bold and said whatever he wanted to say. He finally dropped out of school to run the streets because no one ever took an interest in what he could really be. The ending of this story is not a happy one. Darnell is now locked up because he said "I ain't no punk!" He tried to fight an officer, a fight he lost when he said he was going to show the policeman who was really the boss. This story is so sad because it did not have to turn out that way if someone would have just shown proper interest in Darnell when he was in third grade.

Darnell seriously hurt two of the officers in the scuffle. Although he lost the fight, I was surprised he lived. I visited Darnell at the prison, and while there I asked him if he understood what had happened to him. He said, "I don't know, man, things just got out of control."

I was sad to see another African man end up like Darnell. I wanted to help him escape the prison, but I knew that doing so would only get us both into trouble. I asked Darnell from behind the cold bars why he would try to fight police officers, especially considering the fact that he was outnumbered. He explained to me that where he was from, you just don't let the cops have their way with you. In fact, he said, "...you don't let nobody get crunk on you like that or else people will see you as just a punk." I asked him why he felt he had something to prove to people. He said he didn't have anything to prove to nobody but himself.

An Important African Story

So I went on a journey. I was so confused and saddened by Darnell's self-destructive behaviors that I visited his first grade teacher hoping for insights that might give me some historical perspective on Darnell. I asked her if she saw any signs that Darnell was going to end up the way he did. She told me that when he was in first grade, he was just as well-mannered and behaved as any first grader. His second and third grade teachers reported normal behavior as well. The three teachers and I got together one afternoon for lunch, and I asked them what they knew about Darnell. They proceeded to tell me about his mother and his siblings. I heard stories about the challenges that Darnell had faced throughout his life. I learned a lot about Darnell's personal history that day over lunch. The teachers had done an excellent job of keeping a record of Darnell's personal past. I commended the teachers for having such extensive knowledge of Darnell's personal history. Then I asked them what they knew of Darnell's cultural history.

I said to them, "Well, we know that his personal life was a troubled one, his family was struggling, and he did not have a lot of people to look up to as role models. But what about his strong cultural history? Did you ever focus on that?" The teachers all looked at me with a distant puzzled look as if to say *how on earth is Darnell's cultural history relevant?*

It has become crucial that educators have more than a working knowledge about African children's cultural history for a few critically important reasons. First, knowing the cultural history of African people equips teachers with the necessary tools for combating the negative ideas that continue to surface about Africa. And regardless of how much a person may think that Africa has nothing to do with Black people in the U.S., it is obvious to the rest of the world that Blacks in the U.S. are Africans.

Second, familiarity with African epistemology affords teachers increased pedagogical diversity. But third and most importantly, knowledge of African cultural cosmology plus a working chronological knowledge of African history can allow educators an opportunity to reach African children and to boost them when their personal lives and realities become burdensome. That is, if the child knows his/her cultural history, then he can "fall back" on that when challenged by the fact that his personal life is quite disturbing. For example, if a young person's reality is that his father and brothers are in and out of jail and his mother is struggling to make ends meet, even though those family trials are occurring, he can say, "I am part of the Akan people. And we have a long history. Our history is not one of going to jail and struggling to eat, but it is one of being brave warriors who are great family men." In other words, the child realizes that he is not "bad" but that bad things simply happened within the family. In that same way, a Jewish child might believe that she is unattractive or not very creative, but *still* the child can relish the fact that "I am Jewish, and I am part of a group of people who have overcome great obstacles. I am great."

So I decided that it might be a good idea for someone like Darnell to realize that he is not on an island just floating around with major personal problems. I wanted him to know that he is part of a people with a great cultural history and heritage. I did not know where to start the story of Darnell's cultural journey, so I decided to just start at the beginning.

Darnell Meets Mama LuLu

It is difficult to know exactly when the first of us walked on the planet. However, anthropologists discovered the remains of an early hominid, *Australopithecus afarensis,* whom they nicknamed "Lucy," but since Lucy is a European name and the bones originated 3.2 million years ago in Africa, I have renamed her "Mama LuLu." Mama LuLu's bones were found in Ethiopia by a white anthropologist named Donald Johanson. Johanson and other noted

78

anthropologists believe that Mama LuLu is the "mother of us all." That is, they believe that Mama LuLu represents the origin point for all humanity.

It is important that African children understand that their historical story begins way before some plantation in the United States. In fact, if Mama LuLu is the mother of us all, then she certainly is Darnell's predecessor. I asked Darnell's teachers if they knew that Darnell's history stretched back over 3 million years. They said no.

I showed Darnell a picture of his oldest ancestor. I explained to him that there is an evolutionary relationship between him and Mama LuLu. He smiled when I showed him the picture of her bones. I told him that she was his great, great, great, great, great, great, great, great, great ... grandmother! He turned the picture, tilted his head, lifted his eyebrows, grinned, and opened his eyes real wide. I could see him filling with air. I became excited when I saw Darnell turn from deflated to inflated.

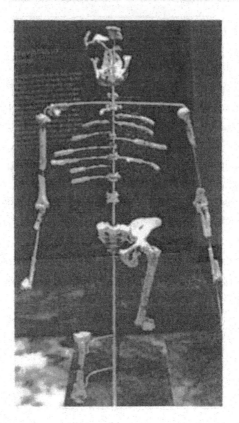

I had told a friend of mine that I was going to visit Darnell at the prison, and he said, "Brother Kmt, I know you! You need a weapon before you go there!" I looked at him curiously. He handed me something that had I not received it from him, things between Darnell and I would have probably always been awkward. Before leaving the prison, I handed Darnell the gift created by my friend. I did not say anything to Darnell. I just gave him a piece of paper, indeed a weapon, that said:

Dear Darnell:
I am an African, and so are you!
I am a descendent of Mama Lulu.
I am part of the richest history in the world,
More valuable than diamonds, gold, and pearls.

An Important African Story

African history stretches back over a million years,
And it's filled with challenge, triumph, and royalty—the
picture is so clear.
I come from great people and some even sat on thrones:
Narmer, Hatshepsut, and the list is quite long!
I'm from the land of great cultures and the world's finest gold,
Where the answers to some amazing things we did ... are
still largely Unknown.
The institution of slavery tried to kill our pride,
But you can't kill an African's will, it just won't die.
Ask Ben Carson, Michael Jordan, or Frederick Douglass
would they quit, Ask Sojourner Truth, Steve Biko, or Bill
Cosby; they're all hits!
When things get tough and you no longer want to try,
Know you have royalty on your inside.
So, Darnell, as you sit here, let your brain boil and stew,
And when you get out, you'll know there's greatness inside
of you.
As you think of the great things you are going to do,
Remember, I'm an African—and so are you!

I told Darnell's teachers about his encounter with
Mama LuLu. Most of them were unaware of who she was,
and when I told them, they also understood their own
relationship to the ancient African woman. Most of them
were surprised that Darnell was so "lit up" by knowing his
great, great, great ... grandmother. I explained to them a
concept that is well-known by the Akan of western Africa:
The importance of the *Hybea* (pronounced shuh-be-uh),
which literally means the written record of one's family
history. The Akan believe that knowing one's cultural history
is the first step to gaining personal power. I told Darnell's
teachers that Mama LuLu's bones were found in Ethiopia
near the Olduvai Gorge region. I explained to them that Black
children get very excited when they learn about themselves
via African history.

Olduvai Gorge region, near Ethiopia

Ms. Jenkins and Ms. Smith (two of Darnell's elementary school teachers) were surprised when I told them that the very region where Mama LuLu's bones were found is known as the "Cradle of Civilization." I told them about anthropologists such as Louis Leakey, Donald Johanson, and Cheikh Anta Diop, all of whom have carefully demonstrated African historical anteriority. I explained that the first family systems were in Africa (Clarke, 1993). I emphasized that point by telling them how there was no such thing as "family" until African people developed the concept of family. I asked them if they thought Darnell needed to know that aspect of his cultural heritage. They all agreed that he could have benefited from knowing that he came from a line of people who developed and invented the concept of family.

Africans were the first on record to develop ways to feed and clothe themselves. Hunting and gathering systems were developed on the African continent. Of course it would follow that Africans would have developed such things considering the fact that they were there early on and had to find ways to meet their basic needs. Darnell should know that in him runs the blood of those who literally "made a way out of no way." He needs to know that his people were not a trivial people—they did develop stop lights and peanut butter (which is great!)—but rather they developed humanity from the start. Both Ms. Smith and Ms. Jenkins wondered how they could use the information to teach their classes. I

An Important African Story

provided them with photos of early Africans developing hunting and gathering systems:

Early Africans were the first to hunt, gather, and develop the concept of family life.

Africans were also the first to develop music and medicine.

Jembe drum

Finger piano

Healing dances

I showed Darnell the same pictures I had shown his teachers. I told him how African people had developed family systems, music, hunting and gathering systems, and medicine. I told him that he was part of the African world community of people with immense creative genius. I explained to him that he was just as much an African as the people who were born and raised in Ghana or Sierra Leone. I told him that he did not have to seek permission from anyone to be African—that he was African by virtue of his birth.

We discussed the Middle Passage, the travel period when Africans were being taken from Africa to other places such as the Americas. He had questions about migration, and he wondered if that was the first time his African people had moved from one place to another. Africans migrated from the Great Lakes region to points north such as Egypt. Darnell said that he had heard that the Egyptians were Black. I told him that the original name of Egypt is Kmt. He said, "That's your name!" I told him that my mentor named me Kmt, which literally means "Land of the Blacks." Darnell wanted to know why the name was changed from Kmt to Egypt. I explained that the ancient Kemites (early Black people of Egypt) had battled with Asians and Europeans and had actually won most of the battles, but after centuries of fighting, they finally began to lose. And when they did, the names that Africans had decided to call things were changed by those who had beaten them.

Darnell was surprised that Africans had actually won most of the battles. I had to explain to him that even though Africans appear to have lost a great deal at this moment in history, they were actually sovereign, independent, and in control of their destiny throughout most of human history. I was very clear with Darnell that although things in Africa were not perfect during the time of the migration from Mama LuLu's region to the region of ancient Kmt, Africans were happily in charge of themselves, albeit with frequent interruptions for battle with Europeans and Asians.

Since Darnell enjoyed learning about periods of African greatness, I decided to tell him about the world's first King of record, a man named Narmer. I told him about how great a warrior Narmer was during his time, called Dynasty 0. I explained to him that King Narmer lived long,

long after Mama LuLu. Darnell was excited because he thought he resembled King Narmer. He does!

King Narmer

Darnell said he understood that the ancient Africans of Mama LuLu's time came long before King Narmer. He was appreciative of the fact that he had seen his great, great, great, great ... grandmother, but now he felt as though he had also gotten to see his great, great ... grandfather—Narmer! We began a conversation about the many great things his people did when they were largely located in eastern Africa.

He said that he had heard of the great pyramids before, so I showed him a photo of one of the first pyramids ever built, called the Step Pyramid. He was very impressed by it after I told him that it was built by his African people during the Third Dynasty (about 2800 B.C.). Darnell gasped. We did the math and found that the Step Pyramid was built nearly 5000 years ago and is still standing. We marveled at the great mathematical genius of African people.

The Great Step Pyramid

One thing Ms. Jenkins was right about is that Darnell is extremely inquisitive. After I showed him the photo of the Step Pyramid, he said, "It looks like a triangle." I said, "right."

He laughed and said, "I guess they knew their geometry!"

I said, "Of course they did."

When I told Ms. Jenkins (Darnell's third grade teacher) about his triangle comment, she said, "Well he's a regular Pythagoras!"

I raised my eyebrows in wonderment. I replied to Ms. Jenkins, "Now you do realize that the first pyramid was built in 2800 B.C., and Pythagoras was born in about 596 B.C.?"

Ms. Jenkins and I did the math and found that the Africans knew about the theory of the squared hypotenuse some two thousand two hundred years before Pythagoras was even born.

Ms. Jenkins teaches seventh grade now. She said, "Well, then, do I tell my students that there *is* no Pythagorean theorem?"

I answered, "Ms. Jenkins, how could the Africans have built the Step Pyramid without vast and extensive knowledge of the theorem that is credited to Pythagoras?"

She looked a bit saddened, that is, until I unveiled a photograph of someone she could tell her students about. I confidently told her that she could safely tell her students that the historically accurate person to whom such a theory should be credited is Imhotep, who was born during the same era as the construction of the Step Pyramid (2800-2600 B.C.). She asked where he was from, and I told her that he was a Black man from Kmt, Africa.

An Important African Story

Imhotep
Architect of the Great Step Pyramid

A couple of days after Ms. Jenkins and I spoke about Imhotep, I found out that she does her homework! She had looked Imhotep up on the Internet and found a few related texts. She found two excellent books that discuss Imhotep: Dr. Yosef ben Jochannan's *The Black Man of the Nile and His Family* (1972), and Anthony Browder's *Nile Valley Contributions to Civilization* (1992). She also found out that Imhotep is considered to be the world's first multi-genius who developed mathematics, medicine, and philosophy. I saw something different in Ms. Jenkins after she uncovered the information about Imhotep. My feelings about her had been quite different up until that time. The Ms. Jenkins I recalled was always busy. I thought about her relationship to Darnell when she had him in the third grade.

You know what's so sad in this story about Darnell Lumpkin? It's that deep down he really wanted to effect change in something. Change in medicine, change in law, and change in the things he saw on a daily basis. The problem was that for the changes he wanted to bring about, he needed someone to bring out what was inside of him—his passions, his dreams, his core beliefs. To come about them completely on his own was too phenomenal a feat.

The one person he trusted and believed could make him a leader, was the one lady he respected most, Ms. Jenkins, his third grade teacher. But Ms. Jenkins had some problems of her own. She was always in everyone else's business and couldn't leave well enough alone. "Honey child this" and "Honey child that" and "Girl, I heard all of Mrs. Jackson's kids gonna be held back!" And she said that the next teacher better pray because next year she was moving up to teach the seventh grade.

Ms. Jenkins knew the 4-1-1 on everyone's class in the school and supposedly what they should be and what they should not be doing. She was so caught up in everyone's business and not leaving well enough alone, that she was paying too much attention to the other classes and not enough to her own. She thought she was doing her best to teach her students to write and read, but she didn't realize that she wasn't giving them all they needed. What Darnell and his peers needed—way more than anything else—was something they didn't even know they were missing: a strong sense of self.

Where did Darnell come from? I mean, what were his beginnings? Had his people been more than slaves and Southern pick-a-ninnies? How would it change him—whenever his light got dim—if he knew the first humans on the planet Earth looked just like him? What if he knew his history didn't start over here, but that it stretched back to Africa over 3 million years? How would it empower him if Ms. Jenkins taught him that the first documented human beings on the planet were Black! What if they taught him who really created science and math and that young Blacks were looked to as leaders and not just as being bad.

It would have helped Darnell tremendously if those things were taught to him. But more importantly, it would have pushed all that's inside of Darnell Lumpkin out!

I am hopeful that Ms. Jenkins is now a new person——she seems to have a new demeanor. She asked me why she had not learned more about the important aspects of African history that we had discussed together. I told her that I believed the U.S. educational system was not geared toward providing information that would help people of African descent understand who they are culturally.

She agreed, and she told me that when she went to her principal and asked about doing a presentation on Imhotep to the faculty so that they could use information about him in their classrooms to help motivate their Black children, the principal said that Imhotep was not in the standardized curriculum. I helped her find a way to re-present the information to her principal by tying Imhotep directly to the curriculum by creating "Imhotepian Units of Geometry," which tied geometry back to its inception and focused students not on the politics of mathematics but instead on the cultural imperatives that go toward furthering Black education. We emphasized the fact that young people can make a contribution to the field of mathematics as opposed to simply being consumers of math

The presentation was excellent and her principal commended her for going the extra mile for the children. I was so glad the teachers did not complain about not knowing how to "implement the cultural piece" into their curriculum. It is disheartening when teachers do not understand that it is about re-Africanization, not simply remaining the same while you try to change students with "the cultural piece." I was elated!

Ms. Jenkins told me that she regrets not having gone to a Black college for her education. She said, "Maybe if I had attended an historically black college or university, I would know all these things I need to know to inspire our children." I explained to Ms. Jenkins that many of the leaders in Black colleges feel too intimidated by the power structures to allow for much African culturally uplifting information. I was encouraged by her tenacity though; she said she was going to find out as much about it as she could so that she could be properly equipped to reach her students.

Ms. Jenkins and I both thought about ways we could encourage teachers to perceive the information about Africa as important cultural knowledge for Black students as opposed to "that 'ol Black stuff," which she said she used to call it. She was a bit perplexed that even after graduating from an Ivy League institution, she still did not have a cultural story for children of African descent.

Ivy League institutions may be rigorous intellectually, but they do not require any rigorous study of people of African descent. One day after school while I was at her school for a meeting, Ms. Jenkins became just too inquisitive about what she had and had not learned at her Ivy League university. So she called one of her education professors and asked him about Imhotep; he said he had never heard of him. She asked him about the great African migration from the Great Lakes region to ancient Kmt, but he had never even heard of Kmt.

I whispered into her ear and said, "Okay, ask him if he knows about the world's first university." He knew nothing of it.

After she got off the telephone with her professor, she had a puzzled look on her face. She said to me, "Now even if he *had* said the right name, Professor Shockley, I would not have known the world's oldest university!" I told her about the University of Ipet Isut, the world's oldest, which was founded in Africa. Her jaw dropped.

She said, "Let me see that picture!" I showed it to her.

The University of Ipet Isut at Waset

An Important African Story

I asked Ms. Jenkins if she would be willing to take a trip to the prison with me to see Darnell. After learning so many new things, she hesitated, saying to me, "I'm going to admit something to you, Dr. Shockley, that I didn't ever think I would say out loud. I have been a very catty teacher. I kind of feel partly responsible for Darnell being there now. If I had known more about who he is culturally when he was in my classroom, maybe he would have been inspired by some of these things and it could have helped him stay out of trouble." I explained to her that she needed to read Gary Howard's book, *We Can't Teach What We Don't Know* (1999). She smiled, and we left to see Darnell.

When we arrived at the prison's visitation area, I saw Darnell approaching while waving something in his hand. His mouth was wide open and he was very, very excited. He paused a minute and said, "Oh, hi, Miss Jenkins." She wiped a tear from her face and said quietly, "Hi, Darnell." I welled up on the inside.

Darnell said, "Dr. Kmt, I have something I found in class!" Ms. Jenkins and I were both curious about it. He continued, "Look, I found something about a great pharaoh who was the last to stave off European and Asian invaders from Kmt! Look!"

I looked at the photo he had, and it was a stately picture of King Ramses II (1279 B.C.)—the last great warrior king to rule Kmt. Ramses II was very well respected during and after his reign. I told Darnell that Ramses II was a good example of how a man can be great, but that a man must also realize that he is only human. I told him something about Ramses II's vanity—the great number of statues of him all over Kmt, his fierce rule, and his deification of himself.

Darnell said, "So he was the HNIC!" I replied that Ramses would never have referred to himself with the "N word." Even the thought of it made Darnell and Ms. Jenkins laugh.

Ramses II

I noticed that Darnell had another paper. He recalled our conversation about the mathematical genius of African people and said, "Dr. Kmt, you ain't the only one who can find out stuff about African history. I got some information *and* a picture of the Great Pyramid of King Khufu!"

I was struck by the beauty of the pyramid. I asked him what was so important about the structure. He said, "Well, it was built during the time around Imhotep's life." I was amazed.

Darnell continued, "It is the largest pyramid built. It's over 480 feet tall and has stood for over 5,000 years but some say over 8,000 years. No cement was used to construct it. Africans just used their minds and were able to build it on pure genius alone, like you always say! It is the first of all of the Seven Wonders of the World." He showed me the picture of the Pyramid of Khufu.

The Great Pyramid of Khufu

An Important African Story

I realized that day that I would be connected to Darnell for a long time. He was learning from me, and I was learning some very valuable lessons from him, namely, that none of our children is a "throw away" person. They all have the desire and ability to learn. They love learning about African history, and as much as some adults may think it is not important, the children light up and become inspired and excited to learn about that history. I also learned that many of my friends who are already African centered need to know Darnell's story so that they can realize that it is not about having mounds of knowledge piled up in your brain but rather about how you use that knowledge to help our children and our communities.

As I was driving Ms. Jenkins back to her car over at the middle school, I remembered that she had been a little emotional, so I asked her what she was thinking about when she first saw Darnell in the jail jumpsuit.

She said, "All I could think about was what if, what if, and what if." She continued, "What if more of us had taken the time to work with Darnell when he was younger. I never thought that knowing I was *African* could make so much of a difference. You know? It's just words."

I agreed that they were words but added that they were very powerful and meaningful words that positively impacted identity issues.

Ms. Jenkins said, "But Kmt, let me ask you this: Okay, so Darnell is so inspired by Ramses II, Imhotep, and Khufu, what about my 'lil girls though, Doc, they need something too?" She laughed, "Did Mama LuLu have any powerful young women who were around in ancient Kmt?"

It was a question I could not have crafted any better than Ms. Jenkins had done herself. I told her about Mama King Hashepsut. She scoffed, "What you mean, 'Mama King'?"

I said, "Well, let me tell you about Hatshepsut." She listened closely. I explained that Hatshepsut was the very first female ruler of the great land of ancient Kmt. I went on, "When Hatshepsut's brother, King Thutmose II, died, she did not allow Thutmose's son to take power. Instead, she took over. She said that Amun Ra (God) made her, not queen, but king! Hatshepsut was in power for 20 years, and during that time she was *king*. Kmt flourished in many ways––financially, the ongoing building of temples, restorations, etc. I believe that Hatshepsut was the world's first womanist! She expanded trade in the region and was also a great warrior. Unfortunately, Hatshepsut always had to appear as a man in order to command respect from her followers."

Mama King Hatshepsut

Back at the school, I explained to Ms. Jenkins and Ms. Smith that after King Ramses II, Kmt began a steady decline as a result of two things: (1) weak leadership after Ramses II, and (2) overconfidence in their ability to remain a cultural giant, and instead of remaining culturally defensive, they began to allow Europeans, Asians, and Arabs freer entrance into their lands. Eventually, the Europeans (such as the Ptolemy family, which includes Cleopatra) were able to dethrone the Africans and make themselves the new kings and queens of Kmt, beginning around 284 B.C.

After becoming the new kings and queens of Kmt, Europeans such as Alexander the so-called Great (hereafter referred to as "Alexander the Greek" because he was a key

An Important African Story

player in European rule) destroyed many longstanding African artifacts (such as great libraries, and many historians (such as Clarke (1993) and Browder (1992)) point out that Napoleon and his soldiers knocked the noses off the statues in ancient Kmt in order to de-Africanize the statues in "phenotypical favor" of the new European rulers.

Many historians say that the Europeans (who were new on the scene and became pharaohs well after ancient Kmt had already been developed through Maat, pyramids, and Imhotepian ingenuity) wanted to take credit for all that had been accomplished prior to their rule. The only way they could do so was to build new temples with European features and begin to lie about the unbelievably awesome dynastic periods of accomplishment from Narmer to Ramses II.

The steady and relatively slow decline after Ramses II was accelerated by Alexander and the Ptolemaic rulers who followed. The Europeans changed the name of Kmt to Aigyptos and altered almost of the African names (such as Ausar, Aset, and Heru—names of Kmt deities) to European names (Osiris, Isis, and Horus).

Alexander the Greek

Alexander the Greek pillaged libraries in ancient Kmt and destroyed many of the cultural artifacts developed by African people.

Napoleon   Her-em-Akhet

Historians point out that Napoleon blew the nose off of Her-em-Akhet. Some believe he was trying to distort the cultural lineage of Her-em-akhet. He may have permanently defaced the African sculpture, but the high cheek bones tell the lineage!

The African Story Continues: A Second Great Migration

I told Darnell about the transition period when Africans lost their rule of Kmt and Europeans took over (later in history the Arabs would assume power and change the name from Aigyptos to Egypt, which is the current name). He asked me if that is when slavery began. I said no. Hamet Maulana (1992) explains that once Africans began to lose very badly to Europeans in ancient Kmt, they scattered and populated other parts of Africa in large(r) numbers. Many of the Kemites moved westward into what is now known as West Africa.

Darnell said, "You mean like when the white man made the 'Indians' go to reservations, just like that, he made the Africans go to western Africa?" I had never thought of the comparison, but it appeared very true. The Africans were unable to remain in eastern Africa because of the problems they were having with Europeans and other cultural groups in the same way that the natives of the U.S. had to revert to reservations.

96

Darnell looked off as though he were trying to imagine what the migration would have been like. I said, "What are you thinking about?"

He said, "Naw, I was just thinking about how I wouldn't have left. I would have stayed there and fought until we could beat them."

After he said that, I thought of teachers. I wondered if the type of comment he had just made was the kind of sentiment that teachers seem worried about transmitting to their students if they tell a truthful historical story. I wondered if I was maybe being too "raw" with Darnell.

Later, I called my mentor, the late Dr. Asa Hilliard, and asked him what he thought. He said to me, "Well, brother Kmt, currently our children have *no* fire about their cultural lineage because they don't know it. Now, you can choose to tell Darnell the story in a way that won't excite and arouse him if you want to, but instead, I would advise you *not* to lie."

I thought about what he said to me for days. What Dr. Hilliard was telling me, in effect, was that there is no way to dampen the story without lying. I empathized with classroom teachers in that moment. I prayed about it, and in the end I had to do what I am advising teachers to do—tell the truth in spite of how you or others feel and channel the African child's energy toward productive Black nationalism. It simply is not fair to miseducate African children in the name of the comfort and convenience of others.

After really thinking about Darnell's statement that he would have stayed and fought those who invaded their territory, I reached the conclusion that it was actually a healthy, sensible impulse to stay on and fight. I thought to myself, "Well, what is the alternative?" You cannot reason with people who are killing you and raping your culture; you can either fight or you can confer power. It was not that Darnell had said anything "radical," it was that I, in my older age, had likely become more inclined toward pacification.

Wanting him to think about our struggle more like an older person is unreasonable and oriented toward generational suicide. Yet, dampening out the warrior in our young people is not the answer. I told Darnell that had he been around to fight for his people, maybe things would have been different. He poked his lips out, slowly nodded his head as if to say, "Oh yea," and looked down as though in deep thought.

As I was trying to read Darnell's mind, to my surprise Ms. Smith and Ms. Jenkins walked in to visit him. I was very happy to see two of his former teachers walk through the door. Ms. Jenkins said excitedly, "Professor Shockley, what are you doing here?" I told her that Darnell and I were discussing our favorite subject—East African history.

She said, "Well, Ms. Smith and I found out some things about West Africa that we thought would also give Darnell a sense of his cultural story." I was impressed with their timing. It was time for a transition to West African history because Darnell and I had just discussed the migration. Ms. Smith handed Darnell a picture of one of West Africa's greatest accomplishments: the University of Sankore at Timbuktu.

Ms. Smith said, "Prior to slavery and colonialism, the University was well-known for its scientific accomplishments, and people from all over the world traveled there. It had become one of the most accomplished institutions of higher learning in the world." She told Darnell that the University still has unexplored archives of information just waiting for him to go and unearth.

Darnell said, "You mean when we got to West Africa, we still had it goin' on?" The three of us laughed. Ms. Jenkins said, "Oh yea, Darnell, it didn't stop in East Africa."

The University of Sankore at Timbuktu

Ms. Jenkins continued, "...you know as Cheryl [Ms. Smith] and I were looking for this material on the University of Sankore at Timbuktu, I found some stuff about how Africans in southern and western Africa used to dance as a way of healing people."

I cut in and said, "Yea, like the people in the Kalahari Desert region, the Kung people in Burkina Faso. People go to Africa and think all the dancing is for fun, but there are healing dances that are sometimes more effective than the practices of doctors in the West, who always want to do surgery or stick someone with a needle."

Darnell chimed in, "How you gonna heal somebody by dancing?"

I said, "Well, in many African societies there are traditional healers. Traditional African culture is more spiritual in nature—people believe that supernatural powers can heal them—and evidence exists that people have been healed by dance and other spiritual mechanisms."

Darnell said, "Dr. Kmt, okay, you gotta give me something I can find on this at the library tomorrow." He laughed. "I don't know about all this healing dances and stuff!"

I told Darnell that I was glad he was so inquisitive and wanted to find the information for himself. As a starting point, I referred him to Richard Katz's book about healing among the Kung people in the Kalahari region. Katz's book is called *Boiling Energy* (1984).

A healing dance among the Kalahari Kung people

Ms. Smith discussed a trip to Ghana she had taken when she was in college. She said she wished the trip had been more focused on culture, but the tour guide seemed to be more interested in the wild and exotic animals that were there. She said that on her trip to Ghana, she and the majority of the other tourists (all Black people from the U.S.) voted to go shopping at the African market instead of spending time in the villages or at Elmina Slave Dungeon. The slave dungeons along the African coast were the very last places Africans saw before they were shipped to the Americas.

Ms. Smith continued, "Now, I regret that we didn't study the place culturally because had we, I could have brought all that information back to my classroom." She continued, "What I did learn over the course of the past 25 years is that Africans excavated gold and diamonds. I know most of the world's gold and diamonds are in Africa and that a group of people in Mali called the Dogon were the first people in modern history...."

Ms. Smith stopped a moment, looked at Darnell, and said, "Now, modern history comprises things in A.D., after the Lord's death, and ancient history covers things in B.C., before His birth. Most of human history is B.C., *not* A.D." She blinked a long blink, sucked some air, and went back to her story.

"Anyway, the Dogon people were the first people in modern history to very seriously study objects in outer space, you know, astronomy. I did not realize the Dogon had been so crucial to the development of theories about astronomy," Ms. Smith went on. "Now, Darnell, when you go to the library to find Kmt's book by Richard Katz, look up this one too." She wrote down this reference for Darnell to study about Dogon astronomy: Temple, R. (1976). *The Sirius Mystery.* St. Martin's Press.

The Dogon people studied astronomy

Most of the world's gold comes from West Africa

Just as I was sitting there thinking about Ms. Smith's story about the Dogon people, and as I was beginning to wonder if we were loading Darnell down with too much information, Ms. Jenkins said, "You know, Professor Shockley, you are so right about needing a sense of an historical story to grasp onto. When you think about it, if we understand that we are God's children first, it's okay. But then we are Lucy's children, we are also Hatshepsut's children, Ramses' children, the children of those who migrated, the Dogons' children, etc. It's like, now I have a 'bone' to hold onto ... something that makes sense so far as where I, as an African woman, came from. I can begin to see the story."

I replied, "Yea, but don't forget, we are just doing some skeletal parts of the 3.2-million-year-old story. A lot is missing."

Ms. Jenkins said, "But it's okay, because see, that's what I needed. I just didn't know *what* or *who* we were enough to even know where and how to start my own study of the other details. Now, I feel like I have something tangible to focus on, and I have people's names and events in history that can lead me. For now, I can at least offer my students the fact that they are part of a great legacy, and I can actually mean it because I have a sense of our story.

"To be honest, the reason I wasn't interested before was because I thought it was too hard to ever learn all that stuff. I figured I had been fine up to this point, so why do all that reading. But, you know what, it's worth it. It really is worth it."

I thought about what Ms. Jenkins was saying, and I silently thanked my mentors for helping me to gain an understanding of our story. I said, "It is beyond helpful to have an African storyline because it helps us to organize our thoughts and..." I was cut off by one of the guards, a 6' 4", 260-pound African "American" man. I thought to myself, "Here we go. Now he knows we have another 10 minutes of visitation, but he probably just doesn't want to hear what we are talking about anymore."

The guard stepped over and said, "Are you Dr. Shockley?"

I said, "Yes."

He said, "I don't mean to interrupt, but as you know I have been here since you all started coming to visit. I heard how y'awl started with, you know, Ethiopia. My grandmother is Ethiopian. Then y'awl moved from there up through, is it Kmt?"

I answered, "Yea."

He continued, "Then y'awl talked about a migration to West Africa and today y'awl were talking about the University at Timbuktu, right?"

I again said, "Yea."

The big man went on. "Well, what about the great empires of Ghana, Mali, and Songhay?" I raised my eyebrows in total and complete surprise. I was glad he knew that history. He continued, "My grandmother told me about how Africa became a great cultural center for centuries during the empires of Ghana, Mali, and Songhay."

I said, "Unfortunately, Africans were invaded by Europeans who forced their brand of Christianity on us, demanding that we discontinue our indigenous cultural practices, and Arabs did the same thing with Islam."

The guard replied, "Yes sir, that's exactly why we have so many in African countries now who practice Christianity and Islam, but they don't have a sense of their own indigenous culture."

Darnell got into the discussion with, "So after we got to West Africa, we developed three more mighty empires and we still had people coming in and trying to get us to change? Why did they want us to change if we were doing fine all by ourselves?"

I replied, "Well, Darnell, one of the things is that Africans developed a pacifism after the fall of Kmt. Since that time, we have allowed others to enter, and usually without the circumspection we should have had."

Askia Muhammad Toure,
leader during the Great Songhay Empire

Sunni Ali Ber,
leader of the Songhay people

I was sorry that I had made assumptions about what the guard was thinking. All too often I think people of African descent make assumptions about one another based upon our experience with some other person. We have to realize that each person is unique and different, and we should give one another a chance. Assumptions hurt the community. The prison guard actually added a very important missing piece to our discussion. I gave Darnell another reference for readings on the great African empires, a slip of paper that read: Jackson, J.G. (2001). *Introduction to African Civilizations*. Citadel Press.

An Important African Story

After our discussion of the great empires, Darnell said, "Well if people were able to come into Africa so easily, that's probably how slavery got started."

I shook my head "yes" and said, "Exactly, and that's our next turn in the story. Recall all the great migrations—from the Ethiopian regions to Kmt to West Africa?"

Everyone recalled. I continued, "Well, another great migration took place when during and after the fall of the three great empires we became very vulnerable and continued to allow foreigners to enter our African spaces.

"Europeans would come to Africa in the name of friendship, and they used African pacifism against Africans. Eventually, they made Africans slaves right there on African lands. Because Europeans had guns and Africans did not, they were able to force us to do what they wanted. Namely, they wanted us to stop practicing our own cultures, stop speaking our languages, and stop worshipping our own God. They wanted us to practice their cultures, speak their languages, and worship the deity they had presented to us as God."

Darnell questioned, "Why?"

I answered, "Because Europeans knew if they could get Africans to give up their God, their culture, their folkways and mores, and adopt foreign European culture, they could get them to do anything else they wanted them to do. When you do that to a people on their own land, you have colonized them. Africans' minds were effectively colonized."

Darnell looked down and nodded slowly. I could tell that he understood.

Africans continued to trust Europeans as "visitors" even after they lost much of their land. When Africans in Africa tried to revolt, Europeans would threaten them with guns and other harsh reprisals.

Ms. Smith said, "See, and that's where they say our history starts because I know that part. I did learn that at the university! Once they colonized Africans in Africa, they then forced, via gunpoint, Africans to capture other Africans. Those captured for Europeans, were put in holding cells like Elmina Dungeon, which I did not visit when I was in Ghana! And there were plenty of other places along the western and southern coasts of Africa where Africans were in dungeons waiting to be taken to the U.S. and other places in the New World."

Africans were placed in dungeons
like this one at Elmina on Ghana's west coast

While in the dungeons, Africans were treated as though they were not even human beings. Read about the horrific treatment they underwent in the book *Black Holocaust for Beginners* (1998) by S.E. Anderson. Africans were forced onto slave ships after leaving the dungeons. The ships traveled to America and other places where Africans were treated worse than farm animals. They were enslaved.

While many African kings and queens struggled to keep the Europeans from stealing their people, one leader named Queen Nzingha of Ngongo (pronounced Angola by Europeans), was known as a very harsh fighter and led the resistance movement against the Portuguese invaders who were attempting to find Africans in Ngongo for the slave trade. During her reign as queen, she won many battles against the European invaders.

An Important African Story

Queen Nzingha of Ngongo

Slavery was a process of making African minds think exactly as the Europeans wanted them to think so that they could easily control them. During slavery, it was against the law for an African to talk about King Narmer, Imhotep, the University of Ipet Isut, Queen Hatshepsut, King Ramses II, Prempeh I, or Queen Nzingha. Africans were disallowed from having conversations about things that might remind them of their greatness and mightiness If they had been able to talk about such things, they might have realized that they could have beaten the Europeans who held them as chattel slaves for almost 300 years in the United States and throughout the Caribbean.

Enslaved Africans worked
for free from sun up to sun down

The Europeans were very careful to make sure that Africans did not think about their ancestry and went as far as giving every African person a European name so they would break all ties to their homeland. In fact, they said many negative things about Africa so that the enslaved Africans would begin to feel as though it was better to be "American" than African. That is, they wanted the slaves to feel as though they were better off as slaves on American plantations than free and independent Africans in Africa. The process of making Blacks believe that freedom and independence were less desirable than slavery included beating Africans with whips and other harsh instruments whenever they spoke positively about Africa.

The enslaved Africans were beaten when they did not do what Europeans told them to do

After making Africans too fearful to look toward Africa in hopes of returning there, and too slave-minded to even want to practice African culture, Europeans started calling Africans outside of their African names, which severed them from their brothers and sisters back in Africa because they saw themselves as being "different" from their brothers and sisters back home.

For example, many of the people who were forced to come to America and become enslaved were from the Ibo regions of Nigeria. Others were Akan from Ghana, and many were Fante from Ivory Coast and Ghana. But instead of calling Africans by their African names, they were referred to as "niggers." There were no "niggers" in Africa, so if these Africans who were enslaved in America started to believe they were niggers (a.k.a. niggas), the Europeans would have successfully detached them from their own people (which was their goal in the first place).

The European slaveholders defined a nigger as a lazy, shiftless person with no purpose except that of serving white masters. They whipped Africans constantly, trying to get them to believe that they were niggers. It finally worked. Now many "Black" people in the United States still call each other nigger when they are angry with one another, and sometimes they even say it when they mean to imply something nice and endearing.

After I discussed all of the above, Darnell said, "I will never say nigger or nigga again." That would have been music to our ancestors' ears! I could feel it!

Africans vs. Niggers: Re-Africanization and Mental Wars

Ms. Jenkins, Ms. Smith, Darnell, and I engaged in a conversation about how many "Black" people refuse to call themselves African. Darnell said, "Well I used to think of an African as somebody who just ain't up on the technology, runs around in dirty clothes in Africa, and is just simple-minded. Now I can see how that is really the image of all of us in the minds of those who give us no respect."

Ms. Jenkins said, "I see now why we have so many fighters in our community, past and present. She enumerated a few great leaders:

Harriet Tubman, leader of her
people, forced Blacks to recognize
that they were not free. Many of the
slaves argued with her, saying that
they were, in fact, free. She threatened
to kill those who were slave-minded.

Frederick Douglas.
Born enslaved,
he bought his freedom and then worked
to end the institution of slavery.
He did not just say to his people,
"I hope you all find a way." He helped make a way.

Marcus Garvey.
Helped many people make
it back home to Africa.

An Important African Story

Elijah Muhammad.
Founder of the Nation of Islam,
a Black self-help group that helped
raise the consciousness of many Africans in the U.S.

Louis Farrakhan.
Current Leader of the
Nation of Islam who organized the
Million Man March and the
Millions More Movement

I said, "Exactly. And those people were not niggers or niggas, they were African people just like Imhotep and the rest."

Ms. Smith said, "Well, Kmt, I can see that we are Africans, I can see that. *But,* how you gonna convince these *Black* folks that we should stop calling ourselves Negroes and people of color and stuff?"

I told Ms. Smith that one of my mentors said something very interesting to me one day. "He said, 'Most of the names that people use to refer to Black people are nicknames. There is no place on the map where you can find a country called People of Color, Minority Country, The Disadvantaged Nation, or even Black Country. At least the term African American has land affiliation. It's the wrong term, because we are Africans, but it's at least half right.' "

Ms. Jenkins responded, "It just seems so hopeless sometimes. There's no way we can convince the people in this country to start calling Black children, and especially themselves, African, and to learn the story."

I told her that it was not important to convince other people. I said, "They will come to their own understandings in their own time." She looked discouraged. I went on, "When I think about all the things that African people have endured, and I think about the allegiance we pledge, not to ourselves but to our oppressor, and then I keep thinking and thinking and thinking about how all of this is difficult to swallow and how Africans in the Western Hemisphere are engaging in identity genocide, I always come back to what psychiatrist Dr. Frances Cress-Welsing says is the most healthy way to intake all of this madness. She said just think about all of it, help try to figure out ways to make it better, then look up and say 'That's interesting!'"

I continued, "I think it's important that we not allow ourselves to feel overwhelmed by all of this because that feeling itself is a weapon against our forward progress." Darnell shook his head in understanding.

Ms. Smith said, "You know, I know Frances Welsing, and I think I like her suggestion. It's interesting! How about that! It's just interesting, isn't it?" Ms. Smith had a satisfied look on her face. I knew that our discussion time was just about complete, there at the jailhouse.

Darnell said, "Thank y'awl, but you know what, it's like we are at war or something and don't even know it."

I said, "Darnell, what do you mean?"

He continued, "I mean, if everybody like the Europeans, the Arabs, even Christians and Muslims, you know, if everybody wants us to do something different just because they don't want us to *be* who we is..."

Ms. Jenkins stopped him: "Are!"

Darnell continued, "Oh, yes ma'am, who we *are*, then maybe the answer to us winning this thing is us doin' just that—bein' who we are!" Darnell did not seem much like a special education student anymore!

I said, "Darnell, your statement is brilliant! If Baba Kwame Agyei and his wife Mama Akua Nson Akoto were here, they'd say something to the effect of how the brilliance really lies in our young people. In Baba Agyei and Mama Akua's [1999] book *The Sankofa Movement*, they argue for exactly what you just said."

Darnell did not understand, so I continued. "Baba Agyei, Mama Akua, and others such as Baba Sanyika Anwisye believe that with all that African people lost, the best way for us to regain our minds is for us to reattach to an African culture."

Ms. Jenkins queried, "But how can we do that in this context we live in now. We are not in Africa."

Darnell said, "Hold up, Doc, I got this one!" I conceded and Darnell continued. "It all makes sense now. It's like okay, cool, we've been through all this and from the very beginning the thing we've held onto when we didn't have nothing..." he chuckled, "I mean *anything* to hold on to, is the thing that makes us who we actually are."

I nodded and Darnell continued. He said, "It's like, I can rap and I like boltin' up in my gear and everything [meaning that Darnell likes to wear the latest street fashions], but even though I'm all about the hip hop, I'm *not* hip hop. I'm a African."

Ms. Jenkins corrected, "You're *an* African."

He said, "Cool, yea right, I'm an African. It's like all the old people, no offense, they like wearing their jewelry and getting bolted up to go out to church and stuff like that, but none of that is who we actually *are*. We *are* Africans and obviously there's something about being that that scares other people and makes them want us to be something else. Yea, the power is in that joint right there. Just bein' African."

Darnell inspired me. I said, "Well, the thing that makes people scared about us being who we are is that to regain real power, we have to resurrect ourselves from the malaise we now find ourselves in and reattach to an African cultural framework."

Darnell looked at me with a knitted brow. He said, "I don't know about all that cultural framework stuff, Doc, but I know if we could go back and practice what we used to practice when we were in Africa, and give them back all the stuff they gave us, we would be a force to be reckoned with."

Ms. Jenkins added her thoughts. "Okay, so what you're saying is that all we have to do is be the African people we are, regardless of the fact that, for example, I live on the South Side of town, not in Africa. Anyway, regardless of where we are, we have to know our cultural story and behave like the Africans we are."

Ms. Smith amplified the point. "What that will require is that we not only read and study, but that we take trips to Africa, that we adopt some of the traditional practices. That we stop having so much *fun* with all of the toys and trinkets in *this* society and begin to take what Kmt and Baba Agyei and Maka Akua call re-Africanization seriously."

I said, "And one thing that is so important is that we realize it's not enough to know what it's about..."

I was interrupted by Darnell. "...I know what you 'bout to say! We have to live it. We have to *be* African. We have to be our African cultural selves, right?"

I wished I could hug him, but the pane of glass was between us. Darnell is special. Not special ed.

As we were packing up and preparing to go, I dropped a piece of paper on the floor. Ms. Jenkins noticed and said, "Dr. Shockley, what is that?"

I explained, "It's just something I was pondering about at home the other day, no big deal."

She said, "Wait, let me see that." She quickly read the note, then shouted, "Darnell, look at this!"

He turned quickly, the friendly guard allowing him another second.

Ms. Jenkins said, "Dr. Shockley, let Darnell take this with him."

I indicated no objection, so she handed the paper to Darnell, who turned and started toward his cell.

This is what Darnell received:

The American Journey

1620 _____ Present

This is what Darnell *should have* received:

The African Journey

3.2 Million Years Ago _____ Present

As we started on our way back to the school, I asked Ms. Jenkins why she thought that little timeline thing was so important. She said, "I never realized that most of our history was really not spent in the Americas. We have over 3 million years of history in Africa. When you look at that line, what it says is that we have really only been here for a *very* short period of time." She continued, "Why, then, do we focus so much attention on it?"

Ms. Smith and I both at once said: "It's a war for the African child's mind!" We laughed because we were in perfect unison. We, two very different people, in perfect unison about being African.

Transformations

Ms. Smith, the teacher that taught Darnell, made a decision that she would get some help. She came to the realization that she needed to change, and that her current rate of affecting children just couldn't remain the same. She came to understand that in order to positively impact anyone else, an impactful transition first had to occur within her.

So, she began to read books and study, attend seminars, and she took a trip to ancient Kmt. Knowledge and information became important for her to seek, and her reading and researching slowly changed the way she thought. She changed her thinking, which changed the things she'd say, to herself and to her students every single day. Changing the words she said changed what she did: she stopped gossiping and backbiting and focused more on her kids.

Other teachers would come to her to gossip about another teacher, and she'd say, "Let's go talk to her. Maybe the two of us can reach her."

The other teacher would respond, "I m not trying to start a mess!"

And Ms. Smith would say, "But it's our duty to help her be her best."

So by changing her habits, she came to change her reputation, so that what she was known as before and who she now represented were no longer the same. By changing her character, she became who she needed to be, not just for herself but to impact the children's destinies.

By going through the process, she helped many boys and girls, and Ms. Smith did her part to literally impact the world. She didn't know it at the time, but in one of her classes there sat a now confident little Black boy who could become the first black president.

An Important African Story

Implications

People of African descent (especially in the U.S.) face major social problems, and education is one of those major problems. Many approaches have been employed for helping to find solutions to the education dilemma, but seldom do scholars and practitioners attempt to rediscover that which was lost during the period when people of African descent in the West lost their own self-chosen ways of being. It is unarguable that Blacks in the West face diabolical realities in all areas of people activity. However, functionalist, post-modernist, Afrocentric, and Marxist scholars, although from different perspectives, all offer that education is an activity that is inextricably linked with the culture of the society at large.

Blacks in the West face major moral and cultural dilemmas in all areas of people activity while many Blacks in indigenous sectors of Africa do not face such insurmountable problems. Of course, Africans in Africa do face major problems such as health care and leadership crises. Nevertheless, Africans do not experience threats to the very fabric of their moral existence and major family breakdowns because of cultural vacancy, as do some African-descended groups in the West, such as African Americans.

Clearly, the epistemological, axiological, and cosmological offerings of African culture are reasons why those cultural groups have been able to maintain themselves for many thousands of years without ever facing the kinds of moral and family breakdowns we now witness within African American communities (such as disproportionate crime, economic disparities, miseducation, health and identity crises, African American male extinction, and rampant Black male and female imprisonment). Those breakdowns in African American communities are coupled with an educational system that admits that it struggles to find the desire to teach and reach Black children and scholars and practitioners who admit that they are not sure that the educational system will ever be able to meet the (social, cultural, or educational) needs of Black children/people.

The massiveness of the problem and its historical raison d'être have driven many educationists to the point of exhaustion, so many well-meaning people simply classify African Americans as people of color and advocate for multicultural approaches devoid of utilizable multicultural knowledge. That is, multicultural education is "thrown in" as a solution, but knowledge about the specific groups that make up the multicultural "quilt" is nonexistent.

Even though the popular media have not declared that the African American community is in a state of emergency, some Black scholars, leaders, and organizations have now declared such a state (Akoto, 1992; Kunjufu, 2001). Efforts to "multiculturalize" the curriculum are trivial when they do not include actual usable cultural information. Furthermore, teachers complain that they do not have proper training and curricular materials to employ multicultural educational mandates.

It has become critical for teacher education programs to become authentically multicultural so that teachers are able to offer a wide variety of choices to children, and especially children of African descent, who come from communities that are in a state of emergency. The ethnocentric curriculum has not worked but neither has what Banks (2001) calls the "content integration" method. It is impossible for teachers to offer things to children that they do not know about (Howard, 1999), so multicultural education must be a call for teachers to increase their knowledge of different cultural groups not simply a call to add "ethnic flavor" to the curriculum, such as standardized test scores about Keisha instead of Heather. Such efforts are juvenile and provide no substantive change to ethnocentrism.

The power of Eurocentric education is that teachers are so imbued with Eurocentric perspectives and content that "teaching about other cultures" often unintentionally becomes sitcom-like, starring the Eurocentric perspective with "others" (such as Africans and Asians) as supporting cast. The marginalization of "others" will continue until the call for multicultural education becomes a call for new concrete information about other cultural groups, their ways of being and knowing and their value systems.

As an example, the Akan way of being is a spiritual way. African Americans are descendants of cultural groups of people who valued spiritual things over physical things, that is, they valued the unseen more than the seen. In the African instance, spirituality is knowledge, and behaviors indicate an understanding that energy transfers and action take place on seen (physical) and unseen (spiritual) planes, but the unseen plane is primary. Indigenous African cultural practices demonstrate that human life is primarily a spiritual phenomenon.

African spiritual ontology and epistemology "order" the cultural mandates of behavior within such societies. Akan practitioners even describe the behavioral mandates as being *Nyame Nhe 'HyeE*, that is, they are literally mandates to act "according to God's order." Since the spiritual "orders" the cultural, the cultural is not functional merely in terms of individual utilization. Instead, the culture is functional in terms of its ability to advance communalism. Furthermore, Akan cultural behavior operates not in terms of being self-seeking and individualistic; rather it brings forth a communitarian society that operates via the concept of *azikoazimu* (we belong to each other).

As opposed to operating according to the concept of *azikoazimu*, African Americans have adopted the individualistic cultural ways of knowing found in the Western World, and instead of operating according to the spiritually all-encompassing paradigm of *Nyame Nhye 'HyeE* (God's order), they adhere to the secular/non-secular Western offerings.

African Americans descended from communal/ cooperative African cultures that have worked for African people for thousands of years. Now, as African Americans attempt to compete in Western culture, they find themselves at the bottom of virtually all social tiers for which data is available, including economic, health, and labor disparities and political disenfranchisement. Also, African Americans suffer from rampant miseducation, negative portrayals in the media, and soaring rates of imprisonment among Black males and females. When so many areas are affected, it becomes apparent that the individual problems relate to some larger cultural issues.

Considering the role that miseducation has played in bringing African Americans to the current state of emergency, teachers should become familiar with African ethos so that they can re-Africanize and offer such content options to African American children. The content includes knowledge of how African cultures work, the ways that people interact with one another, the ways that Africans (or certain African groups such as the Yoruba people) think of family responsibility, the African holistic approach to understanding the world, and African cooperative ways of being.

Furthermore, children must know about the things that Africans value, such as the land and interpersonal relationships as opposed to valueless bling-bling. They must know the African conceptualization of what constitutes an honorable man or woman, African conceptions of gender roles, African diet and health, and—most important—they must be educated in ways that help them to conceptualize the world from an African perspective.

It is incumbent upon all of us, but especially people of African descent, to recognize that African children all over the globe are in a state of emergency. We must now put together plans for resolving the emergency, which at this particular time seems insurmountable. But what great undertaking that was ever accomplished didn't.

CHAPTER 5: Where Do We Go From Here?

Mrs. Jenkins and Ms. Smith's stories provide examples of how teachers can use their referent power to maintain the status quo, or they can use that power to inspire change in our young people. Some of the important questions that a story such as Darnell's raises for us is: *What can be done about the large number of miseducated Black youth, considering the fact that (1) There is a shortage of African teachers; (2) Parents are miseducated; (3) You can't build more schools without the finances; and (4) What exactly is the solution to this gargantuan problem?*

Shortage of African Teachers

There are 521,000 Black public school teachers for the nearly 7 million Black public school students. Even though those numbers lend themselves to a 13:1 student/teacher ratio, there still are not enough Black teachers to go around. And what is even more problematic to consider is the problem of how many of the 521,000 teachers are Afrocentric in their thinking. This means that *all* teachers (regardless of race) must know about and understand Darnell's story. The importance of Afrocentric ideology cannot be underscored enough, especially considering some of the information that has been revealed within the pages of this book. Specifically, recall this critical and timely question from the first chapter:

What does it mean for a Black child to perform well within a school system and on standardized tests that are historically and inherently designed to prove and maintain white supremacy?

How do you answer that question? Unfortunately, in many of my interactions with teachers, when I ask that question, they answer with denial and then after my rebuttal, they assert a form of a rhetorical ethic. First, they will imply that my concern is unfounded because "society" has changed and "the tests" and the books/materials are not really biased anymore (denial). Afterward, I rebut with actual facts such as my investigation of the very textbooks that they use and other unarguable evidence such as David Owen's (1999) book called *None of the Above*, which investigates the inherent bias and proves the sheer uselessness of standardized tests. Often the response to that is that *they* teach their students the difference between right and wrong, fact and fiction, truth and lies, and that *their* classroom is different. That response is a personal one, but it is also likely misleading, considering that they first said they believed that the textbooks and the like have "changed." In other words, many teachers unfortunately become defensive when confronted with these matters.

In many instances, some teachers revert to mentioning notions such as replacing white supremacy with "Black supremacy," and/or "concerns" about separatism are unearthed (rhetorical ethic). These concerns are not really addressable because it becomes difficult to gauge the genuineness of a person who suddenly becomes "concerned" about supremacy and segregation when such conditions have existed since America's commencement. To be clear, it seems that a complex mental and emotional process related to questions about race and racism seems to elicit feelings ranging from pseudo-confusion to a "learned" visceral disdain of Afrocentrism. Many teachers find great comfort in rationalizing to maintain the status quo, and in that action, Black children remain uneducated and oppressed.

Hence, the teacher shortage problem is rooted not in numbers but in mentality. There are not enough teachers who are committed to the process of becoming African centered. Teachers must understand that without African-centered education, even if Black students perform well in the (Eurocentric) schools and on the (biased, useless) standardized tests, they are still being educated away from the Black community's interest. Being educated away from one's own interest is a primary reason why so many children of African descent end up in America's prisons and jails.

Since Black teachers are part of the Black community, one would think it should be easier for them to understand the critical importance of the need for major change. Considering the (informal) way that schools work, if Black teachers properly (unashamedly and in an informed way) advocated for Afrocentric education training for themselves and for the families within majority Black K-12 schools, other teachers would support such efforts much more than they do currently.

Recently, I founded the *Nana Baffour African Centered Education Training Institute* (ACETI) in the Washington, DC, area (NanaBaffourInstitute@yahoo.com). This organization is a community training institute that serves to create responsible advocates for African-centered education. Other such efforts are needed in every city throughout the U.S. Without a re-Africanization-focused African-centered education, the Black community will continue on a path toward more material gains for some but less unity and less positive communities for all.

Parents are Miseducated

It should come as a surprise to no one that most Black parents are miseducated about the critical need for Afrocentricity for Black children. There isn't a Black adult alive today who has not been miseducated by white supremacy—regardless of global location. This means that calls for parents to educate their own children only sound good. Global white supremacy has caused difficulty for everyone. Teachers will have to struggle to become more competent about how to successfully reach and retrain the white supremacist system's most popular victim: Black people.

The damage that has been caused by White supremacy (via the enslavement, segregation, lynching, castration, discrimination, police brutality, psychometrical and psychological abuse of Blacks) has primarily impacted Black families in the following ways: (1) Black men and women were never arch enemies until after having been enslaved in the West, and many Black men and women still do not realize that competing groups benefit from their constant bickering; (2) After years of proving the supremacist system wrong, now many Black men have taken on personas that match the dysfunctional behavior that racists have always accused them of having (such as being violent and hypersexual-emotional); (3) Many Black women have become cynical about the prospect of having an opportunity to start families.

The above are symptoms of being miseducated. When an entire group of people are not taught how to use their time from childhood into adulthood, they will turn on each other and become useless to one another. Those may seem like harsh words, but consider that education in the U.S. is mandated up to age 16. Also, there are now a little over 1.5 million Blacks over age 25 with advanced degrees (Congressional Black Caucus Foundation, 2002). All of this education and "...Blacks still own and control less than 1% of the industries in the U.S." (Anderson, 2001). Unfortunately, many Blacks have mistaken "jobs," "nice homes," "fancy cars," and "bling-bling" for worthwhile wealth. Seminars on wealth-building will do nothing to solve this problem. Afrocentric education is the only holistic answer to Black self-hatred and the dissolution of Black families.

Black adults cannot advance their children toward African centeredness until they (the adults) become African centered. However, many Black adults are turned off to

Afrocentric education because they have been trained by the white supremacist "educational" system and media. Following are ways to expose parents to African-centered information: religious organizations, schools (principals should have Afrocentric re-Africanization specialists come to schools repeatedly for transformation programs), and community groups such as ACETI for parents to join.

Establishing Schools and Re-Africanization

One of the solutions that many concerned brothers and sisters have implemented is the installation of new schools, and most of them are charter schools that have tried to establish and maintain an Afrocentric focus. While charter schools are an affordable alternative to more expensive private schools, charter advocates must be extraordinarily careful for the following reasons.

First, a private Afrocentric school is more desirable than a charter school because private institutions have more independence. As a former board member of a charter school that was trying to be Afrocentric, I learned quickly that charter schools are only able to expose the children to the necessary curriculum and experiences to the degree that powerful education bureaucrats are comfortable with, which means that such schools are, by design, institutionally paranoid. The paranoia causes an awkward and virtually unexplainable jousting between two groups: those who are involved with the charter school because they want an Afrocentric education for Black children vs. those who harbor confused or even disdainful feelings about Afrocentrism because they believe that "feel good/seemingly positive" education (like the *mis*education that we all had) is a "privilege" that should not be taken away from children. For example, some confused people point to days like Halloween and state that children are "missing out" when they don't get to have the pretty pumpkins, ghosts, and goblins.

The excuse for jousting often surrounds what "they" believe is acceptable curriculum-wise. "They" are understood to be the powerful white bureaucrats to whom everyone answers. Whereas in a private school people are clear about the curricular mission, purpose, and academic focus, some of the people involved with charter schools are there for financial and/or other reasons, and their involvement often blocks Afrocentric efforts because such confused people often feel inadequate to contribute to those efforts. This confusion leads to chaos.

Second, in some cites charter schools take students away from private schools. Since private schools operate mainly on tuition dollars, when parents opt to save money by sending their children to "Afrocentric" charter schools, it really hurts those private institutions financially. In my experience, I have not seen a charter school that is nearly as effective as the established private Afrocentric schools with which I am familiar. It is understandable, however, that many brothers and sisters want to establish charter schools.

Considering that many parents are not able to afford private schools anyway, charter schools can be better for Black children than some public schools. The reason some may be better is that they can support the Afrocentric focus, whereas public schools are largely not able to be theme-based. But unless the board, administration, and teachers of the charter school are all (or at least a majority) personally re-Africanized and Afrocentric themselves, it would be better for the children and community if such so-called "Afrocentric" charter schools did not exist at all. The children will simply be confused by people who have not made a personal commitment to re-Africanize, which includes choosing an African cultural group to which they will acculturate.

Where Do We Go From Here?

A school where there are African proverbs, sayings, red, black, and green flags, people saying "Habari Gani" and "Akwaaba," people wearing African garb, and students calling the teachers "mama" and "baba" is not necessarily an African-centered school. Such a school can be just as Eurocentric as institutions where no such things take place. A school that is Afrocentric will include all of the above, but most importantly, it will only become an Afrocentric effort when the adults who started the school have decided beforehand to re-Africanize and have attached themselves to the national and/or international community of people who also have re-Africanized.

Finances are an issue, but they are not the most important issue. Re-Africanization is the most important issue. That is, the community would be better off if those who are interested in starting Afrocentric schools and those who consider themselves to be Afrocentric actually made a personal commitment to re-Africanization and made themselves African-centered models for the balance of the African community. With the exception of important (but somewhat optional) travel to Africa, re-Africanizing is not a financial burden.

Perhaps the focus on finances should be shifted from thinking about the burden of dollars needed to the definite commitments needed from those who already say they are Afrocentric. Good models teach the children properly. African-centered models are the only good models for Black children because the Black community needs Afrocentrism, not just positive people with money and job titles. Re-Africanized Africans do not have to worry about being able to finance their projects because embedded in the African culturo-spiritual systems are the ways and means of African productivity. Note the thousands of years of African productivity prior to enslavement and colonization.

Solutions

In the end, the major solution for Black problems (including education) in the U.S. and other places in the world is for Black people to be who they are—and they are Africans. It is no longer sufficient for Blacks to only want to claim their African heritage when they are making a point about all people being African descendants. For example, some will say, "Well, all people came from Africa" as a way to thwart personal responsibility for helping communities fix the problems. Such self-hatred behavior is killing our children and if for no other reason than that, should be stopped.

Existing as Africans cloaked in the culture of Eurocentrism/Americanism seems harmless to many people of African descent. Many people even find the degree to which they personally have become Eurocentrized/Americanized "cute" and/or a matter of personal preference, when such behavior is neither cute nor subject to personal choice.

To illustrate, after conducting an African-centered professional development workshop at an elementary school in Washington, DC, in February, 2008, a teacher said, "So, Dr. Shockley, you're saying that I need to re-Africanize and that unless I teach from an African-centered standpoint, I am miseducating the kids?"

I said, "Yes."

She went on, "So I guess you are also saying that I can't really fully teach that way until I personally become African centered?"

I said, "Yes" again.

She chuckled and said, "Hmmmph! Well, honey, I can't do that 'cause I need my Gucci purse. And honey, I ain't givin' up my Dungy!"

I said, What's a Dungy?"

She said, "Baby, that's my Coach!" She was referring to a designer bag.

While the teacher was entertaining, she meant every word of what she was saying, and what she was saying was that re-Africanizing meant giving up too much Europeanization/Americanization, which she and many other people believe is both fun and sophisticated. While the things she said are obviously colored by humor, when faced with the truth of the need for personal transformation toward Afrocentrism, many people of African descent struggle tremendously with imagining some other way of being.

That struggle manifests with a bit of anger that causes many of them to ask, "Well, will this make me anti-American?" How is being *pro* yourself equated to being *anti* anything?

Our children will continue to suffer until the adults are prepared to sacrifice a bunch of STUFF (often junk) so that we can regain the COMMUNITY.

Bibliography

A List of Useful Reading Selections and References

Afrik, H. T. (1981). *Institutional development: The need for Black educational models and is the community control of schools still alive?* Chicago: Black Spear Press.

Akbar, N. (1984). *From miseducation to education.* Jersey City, NJ: New Mind Productions.

Akbar, N. (1992). *Chains and images of psychological slavery.* Jersey City, NJ: New Mind Productions.

Akoto, K. A. (1992). *Nationbuilding: Theory and practice in Afrikan centered education.* Washington, DC: Pan Afrikan World Institute.

Akoto, K. A. (1999). *The Sankofa movement.* Washington, DC: Okoyo Infocom.

Akoto, K. A. (2001). *What our students need.* Speech given at the annual CIBI Science Exposition, Washington, DC.

Akoto, K. A. (November, 2001). *Imperatives for Afrocentric education.* Paper presented at the annual meeting of the Council of Independent Black Institutions, Trenton, NJ.

Allen, G. (1971). *None dare call it conspiracy.* Concord Press: Seal Beach, CA.

Anderson, J. (1988). *The education of Blacks in the south: 1860-1935.* Chapel Hill: The University of North Carolina Press.

Anderson, C. (2001a). *Powernomics: National plan to empower Black America.* Bethesda, MD: Powernomics Corporation of America.

Anderson, C. (October, 2001b). *The need for Black reparations.* Paper presented at the meeting of the United Black Fund for Reparations, Washington, DC.

Biblioqraphy

Armah, A. K. (1979). *Two thousand seasons*. Chicago: Third World Press.

Asante, M. K. (1980). *Afrocentricity*. Trenton, NJ: Africa World Press.

Asante, M. K. (1988). *The Afrocentric idea*. Philadelphia: Temple University Press.

Asante, M. K. (1990). *Kemet, Afrocentricity and knowledge*. Trenton, NJ: Africa World Press.

Asante, M. K. (1991). "The Afrocentric idea in education." *Journal of Negro Education*, 60, 170-180.

Asante, M. K. (1998). *The Afrocentric idea*. Philadelphia: Temple University Press.

Asante, M. K. (1999). *The painful demise of Eurocentrism*. Trenton, NJ: Africa World Press.

Bell, D. (1992). *Faces at the bottom of the well: The permanence of racism*. New York: Basic Books.

Ben-Jochannan, Y. (1972). *Black man of the Nile and his family: African foundations of European civilization and thought*. New York, NY: Alkebu-lan Books Associates.

Brandwein, P. F. (1981). *Memorandum: On renewing schooling and education*. New York: Harcourt, Brace and Jovanovich.

Brookins, C. C. (1984). A *descriptive analysis of ten independent Black educational models*. Unpublished master's thesis, Michigan State University, Ann Arbor, MI.

Browder, A. (1990). *From the Browder file*. Institute for Karmic Guidance, Washington, DC.

Cabral A. (1970). *National liberation and culture*. Speech given at the Eduardo Mondlane Memorial Lecture Series at Syracuse University, Syracuse, NY.

Cherry, V., Belgrave, F., Jones, W., Kennon, K., Gray, F., & Phillips, F. (1998). "NTU: An Afrocentric approach to substance abuse prevention among African American youth." *The Journal of Primary Prevention*, 18, 3.

Constantine, M., Alleyne, V., Wallace, B., & Franklin-Jackson, D. (2006). "Afrocentric cultural values: Their relation to positive mental health in African American adolescent girls." *Journal of Black Psychology,* 32 (2), 141-154.

Delpit, L. (2001). *Other people's children.* New York: The New Press.

Doughty, J. J. (1973). *A historical analysis of Black education, focusing on the contemporary independent Black school movement.* Unpublished doctoral dissertation, Ohio State University, Columbus, OH.

Fordham, S. & Ogbu, J. (2005). "Black students' school success: Coping with the burden of acting white." *Urban Review,* 18, 176-206.

Hale-Benson, J. (1982). *Black children: Their roots, culture, and learning styles.* Baltimore: The Johns Hopkins University Press.

Hales, M. (1997). *A comparison of the educational progress of African American single sex/same sex, single gender/same gender schools.* Unpublished doctoral dissertation, University of Maryland, College Park, MD.

Harcourt (2008). *Social studies. The United States: Civil war to present.* Harcourt: Orlando, FL.

Haycock, K. & Jerald, C. (2001). "Helping all students achieve: Closing the achievement gap." *National Association of Elementary School Principals,* 82, 20-23 Hilliard, A. (ed.) (1986). *The teachings of Ptahhotep.* Atlanta, GA: Blackwood Press.

Hilliard, A. (1997). *SBA: Reawakening of the African mind.* Gainsville, FL: Makare.

Hopkins, R. (1997). *Educating Black males: Critical lessons in schooling, community and power.* Albany, NY: State University of New York Press.

Hotep, U. (2001). Dedicated to excellence: An Afrocentric oral history of the council of independent Black Institutions, 1970—2000. Unpublished Ph.D. thesis, Duquense University, Pittsburgh, PA.

Bibliography

Iceland, J. & Weinberg, D. (2000). *Racial and ethnic residential segregation in the U.S. 1980-2000.* Retrieved from: http://www.census.gov/www/housing/housing_patterns/front.htm

Johnson, J. & Immerwahr, J. (1994). First things first: *What Americans expect from public schools.* New York: Public Agenda Report.

Kambon, K. K. K. (1992). *The African personality in America: An African centered framework.* Tallahassee, FL: Nubian Nation.

Karenga, M. (1966). *The African American holiday of Kwanzaa.* Los Angeles: University of Sankore Press.

Kunjufu, J. (1995). *Countering the conspiracy to destroy Black boys.* Chicago: African American Images.

Kunjufu, J. (November, 2001). *African American teachers and children.* Paper presented at the annual conference of the National Alliance of Black School Educators, Los Angeles.

Kunjufu, J. (2002). *Black economics: Solutions for economic and community empowerment.* Chicago: African American Images.

Ladson-Billings, G. (1994). *The dream keepers: Successful teachers of African American children.* San Francisco: Jossey-Bass.

Ladson-Billings, G. (2001). *Crossing over to Canaan: The journey of new teachers in diverse classrooms.* San Francisco: Jossey-Bass.

Lee, C. D. (1992). "Profile of an independent Black institution: African-centered education at work." *The Journal of Negro Education, 61,* 160-177.

Lee, J. (2002). " Racial and ethnic achievement gap trends: Reversing the progress toward equity?" *Educational Researcher, 31,* 3-12

Lomotey, K. (1978). *Alternative educational institutions: Concentration on independent Black educational institutions.* Unpublished master's thesis, Cleveland State University, Cleveland, OH.

Lomotey, K. (1992). "Independent Black institutions: African-centered education models." *The Journal of Negro Education*, 61, 455-462.

Madhubuti, H. (1973). *From plan to planet: The need for Afrikan minds and institutions.* Chicago: Third World Press.

Murrell, P. C. (2002). *African-centered pedagogy: Developing schools of achievement for African American children.* New York: State University of New York Press.

National Center for Education Statistics (2004). *The digest of education statistics.* Retrieved 2/15/06 from: www.nces.ed.gov/programs/digest.

Nobles, W. (1987). "Psychometrics and African American reality: A question of cultural antimony." *Negro Educational Review,* 38, 45-55.

Pan African Congress (1970). National Meeting in Frogmore, S.C.

Ratteray, J. D., & Shujaa, M. J. (1987). *Dare to choose: Parental choice at independent neighborhood schools.* Washington, DC: U.S. Department of Education.

Ratteray, J. D. (1990). "African American achievement: A research agenda emphasizing independent schools." In R. Lomotey (ed.), *Going to school: The African American experience,* 197-208. Albany, NY: State University of New York Press.

Ridley, J. A. (1971). *The independent Black (educational) institution: An exploratory study with implications for the institutionalization of American schools.* Unpublished doctoral dissertation, University of Michigan, Flint, MI.

Satterwhite, F. J. (ed..) (1971). *Planning an independent Black educational institution.* New York: Afram Associates.

Shujaa, M. J. (1993). "Education and schooling: You can have one without the other." *Urban Education,* 27, 328-351.

Bibliography

Shujaa, M. J. (1994). *Too much schooling too little education: A paradox of Black life in White societies.* Trenton, NJ: Africa World Press.

Stedman, L. C. (1996). "The achievement crisis is real: A review of the manufactured crisis." *Education Policy Analysis,* 4, 1-11.

Teicher, S. (2006). "An African centered success story." *Christian Science Monitor,* June 8, Tharp, R. G., & Gallimore, R. G. (1991). *Rousing minds to life: Teaching, learning, and schooling in social context.* Cambridge, MA: Cambridge University Press.

Williams, B. (2003). *Closing the achievement gap: A vision for changing beliefs and practices.* Alexandria, VA: Association for Supervision and Curriculum Development.

Wilson, A. (1993). *Awakening the natural genius of Black children.* Washington, DC: Afrikan World InfoSystems.

Woodson, C. G. (1933). *Mis-education of the Negro.* Washington, DC: Associated Publishers.

X, Malcolm (1990). "Message to the grass roots." In G. Brietman (ed.), *Malcolm X speaks: Selected speeches and statements,* 3-17. New York: Grove Press. (Original work published 1965 from speech given November 10, 1963.)

Special Thanks

A special thanks to Mr. L. Kobie Wilkerson for writing some of the poems within this work. You are much appreciated for making such a contribution!